W9-CAT-230

CHECK ✓ LISTS

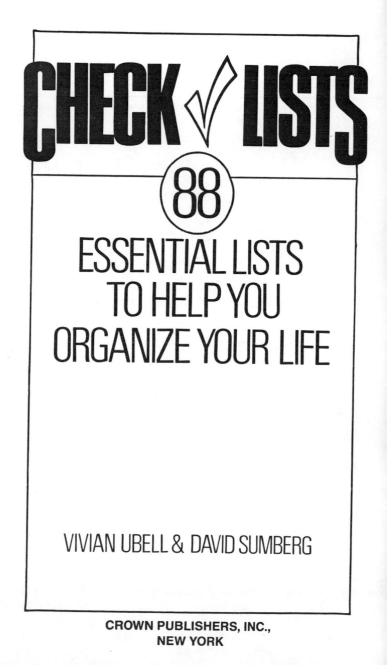

CHECK ✓ LISTS

88
ESSENTIAL LISTS
TO HELP YOU
ORGANIZE YOUR LIFE

VIVIAN UBELL & DAVID SUMBERG

CROWN PUBLISHERS, INC.,
NEW YORK

To Jennifer and Elizabeth
for their patience

Inquiries should be addressed to Crown Publishers, Inc., One
Park Avenue, New York, New York 10016

Printed in the United States of America

Published simultaneously in Canada by General Publishing
Company Limited

Library of Congress Cataloging in Publication Data

Ubell, Vivian.
  Check lists.
  I. Sumberg, David. II. Title.
AC8.U23 1982   081   81-15258
ISBN: 0-517-543680   AACR2

10 9 8 7 6 5 4 3 2 1

First Edition

Contents

Packing Check✓Lists

Social Events Check✓Lists

What-to-Have Check✓Lists

Personal Lists

Acknowledgments

Here is a very special list—the people we would like to thank:

George Bailenson
Susan Breen
Ira Brustein
Te' Chaplain
Pat Clary
The Corley Family
Nicole Cox
Melva Crowell
Peter Dechar
Frances Dropkin
Glenn Firestone
Georgia Franklin
Carole Getzoff
Roger Glassman
Robin Grossfeld
Neil Grossman
Jane Hirshman
Naomi Kleinberg
Ken Koval
Joe and Tracy Marchetta
Ilene Margolin

Bob Norris
Ed O'Connor
Dale Palmer
Barbara Rothberg
Billy Rothberg
Peggy Sandback
David Schochet
Susan Scioli
Barbara Silverman
Steve Simons
Sunnie Singer
Isabel Sklar
Toni Sooter
Jeff Sumberg
Paul and Chris Sumberg
Archie and Shulamis Toder
Jeff Weiss
Margaret Wells
Devorah Zeitlin
Jono Zeitlin
Carol Zimmer
Steve Zimmer

Special thanks to Liz and Jenny for proofreading and for general all around support. Angela Riccardi, our typist, also deserves special gratitude for proofreading as she typed and for the helpful additions she made to many of the lists.

Also thanks to our parents, Harvey and Irene Sumberg and John and Ruth Dropkin, for their help in researching some of the lists or in giving us comments on our progress.

The encouragement of Nach Waxman, our editor, and Hy Cohen, our agent, provided us considerable motivation during the writing of *Check✔Lists*.

Finally, thanks to all our other friends, family, and colleagues who gave us support during the year.

How to Use This Book

We hope that you will be flexible in using these lists and that you'll alter them to meet your own needs. With this in mind, we offer the following general suggestions:

1. Use the blanks in front of each item to write in a check (✔), a cross (×) or a quantity.

2. We've included obvious items on many of the lists, partly because we've found that they are the things most often forgotten. The first time you are camping in the woods without toilet paper should be the last. By being all inclusive, we've tried to dispel your worries about whether we have taken anything for granted.

We've also included many optional items—far more than you'd necessarily want. Suit each list to your needs; just cross out any item you find unnecessary.

3. We have included space on each list so that you can add your own items; blank pages at the end of the book can be used for any special lists you may devise.

4. Most lists, other than packing lists and what-to-have lists, are ordered in a general time sequence. For instance, Moving (list 23) starts with items you do several weeks before the move and leads up to the move itself. Lost Wallet/ Pocketbook (list 11) begins with those steps that need to be taken immediately after the loss.

5. Packing is a very personal activity, and probably most people already have fairly well established mental lists. Nevertheless, the extensive lists offered here may jog your memory and perhaps give you some new ideas. The following are general considerations:
   a. airline restrictions on weight
   b. weight of packed luggage
   c. availability of porters and distance you may have to carry luggage
   d. seasonal needs for heavy or light clothing
   e. laundry and cleaning facilities available
   f. availability of items in country of destination
   g. length of trip
   h. your own style of dress or travel

The Packing lists are arranged by category of item; clothing lists go from inner wear to outer wear. Read the whole list through first and alter the order or organization as you see fit.

6. To keep the book reusable, you can photocopy the lists you need. If you use a regular-size sheet of paper, you'll have lots of extra space to scribble in notes and add extra items.

7. Many lists refer you to other lists. For example, Packing for a Camping Trip (list 58) refers you to Packing for Backpacking (list 59) in case you plan on backpacking while camping. Before You Go (list 40), Travel Arrangements (list 41), and When You Return (list 42) are important references on a number of lists.

8. Please send us, through our publisher, any ideas or suggestions for lists or items you would like to see in the next edition.

Introduction

I often laugh at my urge to make lists, but in fact list making is a great comfort. Once a chore is written down, I can stop worrying about forgetting it. The job doesn't always get done, but I know that somewhere on my list it is there, waiting.

About ten years ago I wrote a packing list for a Cape Cod vacation; when completed, it numbered 311 items. Everything was on it, from bathing suits and beach balls to mosquito netting and curry powder. Friends howled at my compulsion to put everything on paper. Over the years, my Cape Cod packing list, and others I kept, became more and more efficient, and, to my delight, came much in demand from those same friends. Soon they were suggesting that I write a book that would contain my lists. Being agreeable, I duly wrote on my master list, "write list book," where, of course, it stayed . . . and stayed.

When David came into my life some years ago, I was delighted to discover that he, too, was a list maker. Not only was he compulsive about making lists, but—miracle of miracles—he was also compulsive about doing the things he listed. One night, following a long day of worrying about all the chores I had to do in our house, I had a brilliant thought: I would simply transfer some of the items from my list to his. The next morning he woke and, as was his habit, checked his master list. He couldn't believe it. Right there, between his "pay bills" and "get haircut," my "wash windows" had been neatly inserted. He was furious, of course. Not only was he unsettled that his list had been violated but, much worse, he knew he was doomed to do the jobs that had turned up there. He couldn't stand having an undone item messing up the neatness of his finished list. A new life spread out before me. We could pool lists. My liberation was at hand!

From this came a truly major decision: the item "write a list book" was transferred from my list to David's.

Discussions about our list making revealed differences in approach. David likes to put a neat check in front of each completed item, and his lists retain a neat quality for their lifetimes. Mine, on the other hand, quickly look messy and need frequent rewriting because I like to cross out each item after it is completed. For me, crossing off an item is often as satisfying as doing the job itself. (Sometimes, I even list a chore I have already done, just to have the pleasure of crossing it off.) I keep many lists—long-term lists, daily lists, shopping lists, and on and on. The first item on every one is "see lists." My lists have no internal order: "buy car" comes right after "buy tuna fish." David, on the other hand, is very organized: country-house chores have their own section on his list, while city-house chores go elsewhere.

Whenever we travel, David and I invariably debate what is essential to take along and what is optional. He'd like to travel with one suitcase, and I pack three. Every year, as our gear gets gathered for loading in the car for our Cape Cod vacation, he swears it won't all fit, while I swear it will. You can certainly disagree with what we consider essential or optional. If we missed something, let us know, in care of our publishers. If you need other lists, let us know that too, for lists grow and change as they reflect the way our lives change.

VIVIAN UBELL

CHECK ✓ LISTS

1. Finding a Roommate/ Moving in with Someone

You may be the person who's moving into someone else's apartment or you may have the apartment that someone else is moving into. Your relationship with each other—whether you're lovers, friends, or strangers—and your own personalities will help determine just how much structure you'll require to make it work.

___ Write advertisement
___ Tell friends, colleagues, classmates that you are looking
___ Place/read advertisements in newspapers, school bulletin boards, schools, churches, hospitals, bookstores, work places
___ Advertise in speciality newspapers and magazines that reflect your interests
___ Register at roommate agencies
___ See real estate agents
___ Check local laws on cohabitation
___ Check lease for restrictions
___ Read guides on contracts for people living together
___ Make list of important items to discuss: money, food preferences, chores, living habits and schedules, pets, smoking, allergies, parties, guests
___ Discuss joint rules and schedules for cleaning, cooking, shopping, entertaining
___ Discuss finances: who pays rent, phone, utilities, groceries, household furnishings
___ Decide how space is to be divided
___ Decide who gets place if it doesn't work out
___ Decide on length of trial period
___ Decide how to divide joint purchases if you split up
___ Label items where ownership may be confusing: books, records, linens, kitchen items
___ Make written contracts about responsibilities and obligations

___ Check inventory of each house/decide what will be
  stored or used
___ Open joint accounts: banks, utilities, phone
___ Have mail forwarded
___ Call phone company/have calls forwarded to new
  phone number
___ Get dual listing in telephone directory
___ Notify magazines and other subscriptions that you
  have moved
___ Arrange closets and furniture to accommodate new
  person
___ Change answering-machine message
___ Put new names on mailbox and door

SEE ALSO:

MOVING (LIST 23)

ESTABLISHING YOURSELF IN A NEW NEIGHBORHOOD
    (LIST 24)

2. Getting Married

This list may seem overwhelming at first, but so is marriage. Also, you may have many months between the decision to get married and the event itself.

If you are getting married at home, see Preparing a Wedding Party at Home (list 73).

___ Discuss the type and size wedding you want
___ Discuss same with parents
___ Select place and date for affair/reserve place
___ Reserve church, synagogue, meeting hall
___ Select band/hire
___ Select caterer/plan menu
___ Check on liquor, champagne, bartender with caterer
___ Rent needed items: outdoor tent, dance floor, chairs, tables, linens, portable bar, dishes, silverware, bar supplies
___ Check on special religious or family traditions: giving favors to guests, breaking a glass, throwing rice, saying special prayers
___ Select clergyman/discuss wedding plans, religious issues, ceremony
___ Make up guest list
___ Print invitations, RSVP notes and envelopes, travel instructions, thank-you notes
___ Buy stamps/address envelopes/mail invitations
___ Discuss engagement party, shower, bachelor party with family and friends
___ Plan honeymoon/make reservations
___ Reserve rooms for out-of-town guests
___ Select wedding party: best man, maid and matron of honor, bridesmaid, ushers, flower girl, ring bearer
___ Select photographer
___ Decide on responsibilities and financial details with family: who will order and pay for flowers, band, liquor, photographer, clergyman
___ Choose color scheme

- Order accessories with name and date: matches, napkins, ashtrays, favors for guests
- Choose/register china patterns
- Choose/register silver patterns
- Select gowns/arrange fittings
- Order veils, hats, gloves
- Order tuxedos, shirts, ties
- Buy shoes/have dyed
- Hire florist/select flower arrangements, bouquets, flower-girl basket, boutonnieres, corsages
- Arrange to have flowers delivered to home before wedding
- Get pillow for ring bearer
- Select/order cake
- Select/order rings
- Arrange transportation to ceremony, reception, airport
- Choose gifts for attendants
- Arrange bridesmaid luncheon, rehearsal dinner
- Plan wedding rehearsal
- Make list of gifts you'd like to receive and give to family members
- Make seating plan
- Check state laws regarding waiting time between blood test, license, marriage
- Plan program, music for wedding, reception/discuss with bandleader, master of ceremonies
- Discuss toasts with best man
- Make appointment for manicure, makeup, haircut, hair coloring
- Choose witnesses
- Get license
- Get blood test
- Buy miscellaneous personal items: underwear, garter, gloves, cosmetics, hairpins for veil
- See doctor for checkup and birth-control information
- Discuss banking plans/arrange joint financial plan
- Make list of what has to be paid for/have money on hand to pay for services, hall, clergyman, caterer's tips
- Buy rice, confetti, tin cans for car
- Pack for honeymoon

Life's Joys

___ Arrange for transportation of gifts back home
___ Make list of gifts as they are opened
___ Send thank-you notes

SEE ALSO:
FINDING AN APARTMENT (LIST 22)
BEFORE YOU GO (LIST 40)
TRAVEL ARRANGEMENTS (LIST 41)
PREPARING A SHOWER (LIST 72)

3. Expecting a Baby

You have seven or eight months to complete these tasks, depending on how quickly you confirm your pregnancy. For some people the baby will come before they truly feel ready for it, no matter how well they prepare themselves. For others, the waiting seems endless and they welcome the tasks as a way of filling the time while waiting for the birth.

In either case the joys of having the baby more than make up for the exertions involved.

___ Prepare older children for newcomer
___ Discuss/interview doctors, midwives about attitudes and facts on the following:
   a. type of delivery desired: natural, caesarean, induced
   b. hospital affiliations and regulations: can husband be in delivery room, use of a birthing room, photography in the delivery room
   c. anesthesia
   d. natural-childbirth classes
   e. diet, vitamins, milk consumption
   f. medications during pregnancy and labor
   g. sex during pregnancy
   h. weight gain
   i. exercise and body care
   j. genetic counseling and amnioscentesis
   k. breast feeding
   l. circumcision
   m. fees
___ Choose obstetrician, midwife
___ Select hospital/discuss regulations and costs
___ Tour hospital
___ Find out about financial coverage
___ Visit dentist

Life's Joys

___ Read books on pregnancy, childbirth, nursing, infants
___ Arrange for natural-childbirth classes/practice exercises
___ Arrange for child-care classes
___ Buy maternity clothes
___ Interview/select pediatrician
___ Arrange for help after returning home: baby nurse, cleaning help, moral support
___ Arrange child care for older children during hospitalization
___ Decide on room and space for baby
___ Select/order/borrow baby furniture
___ Select/order/borrow baby clothes
___ Order household equipment: washing machine, dryer
___ Choose a name for the baby
___ Arrange diaper service
___ Choose godparents
___ Prepare to terminate at work/apply for maternity or paternity leave
___ Wash/prepare hand-me-down clothes and furniture from older children and others
___ Prepare room for baby
___ Ask someone to get needed drug items, medications, clothing, baby furniture, deliveries while you are in hospital
___ Make list of stores where baby items were purchased/check on delivery schedule
___ Get a haircut, manicure, pedicure, massage before hospitalization
___ Find local stores that will deliver after you're home
___ Pack suitcase and baby items for hospital
___ Do a few things you may not do again for awhile: see a movie, go to a concert, eat out

SEE ALSO:
　PREPARING A NURSERY (LIST 4)
　AFTER THE BABY IS BORN (LIST 5)
　PACKING FOR A HOSPITAL STAY (LIST 68)

4. Preparing a Nursery

This list will almost surely include equipment that you won't find necessary; assess your needs and cross out accordingly. We have not recommended any specific quantities because needs will vary depending on the type of laundry facilities available.

Consult your physician about recommended toiletries and drugs to keep on hand.

Sleeping

— Crib, bassinet
— Crib sheets
— Crib bumpers
— Waterproof dry down sheet
— Blankets
— Receiving blankets

Transporting

— Carriage, stroller
— Car seat
— Back carrier, front carrier
— Walker
— Carriage sheets
— Carriage blanket clips, pillow, pillowcases
— Carriage blankets
— Mosquito netting
— Carryall for day trips

Changing and Washing

— Dressing table
— Changing pad
— Bathtub
— Towels
— Washcloths
— Cloth diapers (a few for burping are advisable even if you use disposables)
— Safety pins
— Rubber pants
— Disposable diapers
— Pre-moistened wipes
— Diaper pail
— Garbage pail

Feeding

— Infant seat
— Highchair
— Feeding dish, spoon
— Food grinder
— Bottles
— Nipples
— Bottle tops, caps
— Bottle brush
— Formula
— Sterilizer

Life's Joys

___ Formula equipment: funnel, measuring cup
___ Bottle warmer
___ Bib

Clothing

___ Stretch suits
___ Kimonos, nightgowns
___ Undershirts, socks
___ Dress outfits
___ Sweaters
___ Sun hat, cold-weather hat
___ Booties, mittens
___ Pouch, bunting, snowsuit
___ Sun suits

Drugs and Toiletries

___ Pacifier
___ Baby soap, soap dish
___ Baby shampoo
___ Comb, brush
___ Powder
___ Lotion, ointment, oil
___ Nail scissors, clippers

___ Cotton balls, cotton swabs
___ Petroleum jelly
___ Thermometer
___ Alcohol
___ Baby aspirin
___ Vitamins
___ Humidifier, vaporizer

Amusement

___ Playpen
___ Toys
___ Rattles
___ Crib mobiles
___ Bath toys
___ Visual objects: pictures, posters, ceiling mobiles
___ Swing

Other

___ Chest of drawers
___ Baby hangers
___ Lamp
___ Night light
___ Rocking chair (for parents)

5. After the Baby Is Born

After the baby arrives, parents may feel both overjoyed and overwhelmed. Postpartum depressions, sleepless nights, and painful incisions are all normal, but are nonetheless difficult to cope with. It often helps either to read about these issues or to talk about them with others. When you know you're not the only one going through it, it feels easier.

— Notify close friends and relatives
— Check religious customs
— Arrange for christening
— Arrange circumcision, *bris*
— Discuss lactation with physician
— Arrange for pediatrician to do one-month checkup
— Select godparents, guardians
— Hire household help
— Buy/borrow needed items: playpen, stroller, carriage
— Print/buy announcements
— Send announcements
— Keep list of gifts as they arrive
— Buy books on child rearing
— Organize day
— Exercise
— Cook dinners in morning
— Take nap
— Arrange time off for yourself
— Set schedule for all involved in infant care
— Find stores that deliver
— Arrange to have others cook occasionally
— Arrange for babysitting
— Write thank-you notes/mail
— Rewrite will/change insurance policies
— Start photo album
— Schedule doctor's appointment for postpartum checkup

6. Adopting a Child

Adopting a child can often be a difficult, complicated process and it may take a long time. Our first item should probably be "have patience."

Many people decide to adopt an older or a handicapped or a foreign child. This list covers tasks for such situations as well.

Not all documentation listed below is required by every agency, so check with each agency about its specific requirements.

__ Read books on parenting and adopting children
__ Discuss adoption with other children in family
__ Talk about adoption with family and friends
__ Discuss/make decision on gender and age of child, ethnic background, handicaps
__ Research local adoption sources (the library is a good place to start)
__ Call federal, state, local governmental agencies for names of adoption agencies
__ Call/write adoption agencies in area/contact steering agencies
__ Ask adoption agency to list you with local, state, national adoption exchanges
__ Contact international adoption agencies
__ Request applications from all agencies
__ Fill out application forms
__ Choose the agencies you will work with
__ Set up interviews
__ Decide on range of children you will accept/discuss with agency
__ Look at pictures of children available
__ Fill out financial application
__ Make copies of W-2 forms, wage stubs, tax returns
__ Obtain copies of necessary birth certificates
__ Duplicate marriage license, divorce papers, death certificates (if widow or widower), baptismal records

- Get physical examination/document all serious medical problems/document course of treatment
- Get copy of medical coverage
- Notify friends and colleagues who can provide written references for you
- Get religious references
- Obtain employment references
- Obtain fertility records
- Make copy of service discharge
- Obtain naturalization and citizenship papers
- Get copies of arrest and conviction records
- Obtain confirmation papers
- Prepare statement of faith
- Notify agency of any prior refusals
- Explore financial subsidies
- Decide where child will sleep/find larger space if needed
- Take family pictures
- Hire a lawyer
- Put together necessary legal papers
- Arrange survivor care
- Write new will
- Get up-to-date medical report
- Notify U.S. Immigration and Naturalization Service/ obtain visa/obtain fingerprint forms
- Ask for reasons in writing if refused by agencies
- Contact local schools about enrolling the new child
- Check availability of day care, babysitting
- Buy gift for child's first visit
- Buy your own children a gift
- Plan first meal with child/find out his or her favorite food
- Take child shopping, to a movie, playground, park, zoo
- Show child his or her bedroom
- Take child to local schools, around the neighborhood
- Purchase/borrow needed items: beds, playpens, dressers, toys
- Buy necessary clothes and luggage
- Find support group for yourself/join preadoption and postadoption groups

___ Arrange visit to child's foster parents to discuss transition
___ Arrange date and transportation to pick up child
___ Arrange playmates and playgroup
___ Arrange child-care network / hire help
___ Check local laws and with lawyer about access to information about background (for you and the child)
___ Contact IRS for tax information on deductions for children
___ Pick up child
___ Arrange medical, dental, ophthalmological exams for child

SEE ALSO:
PREPARING THE NURSERY (LIST 4)
AFTER THE BABY IS BORN (LIST 5)

7. Sending a Young Child to School

___ Register child in school
___ Get school procedures and school calendar
___ Write list of phone numbers where you can be reached/leave at school
___ Take child for medical checkup and innoculations
___ Take child for dental checkup
___ Take child for eye examination/buy eyeglasses
___ Look through child's wardrobe/buy needed clothes, shoes, uniform
___ Ask school for list of required supplies
___ Buy school supplies: book bag, pencil case, looseleaf notebook, paper, pens, pencils, eraser, ruler, protractor
___ Label items which are easily lost: mittens, boots, hats, sweaters, book bag
___ Arrange transportation, car pool, someone to walk with child
___ Arrange child care for after school and lunch/discuss with child
___ Get bus passes
___ Practice going over route to school with child
___ Make lunch plans/buy lunch box
___ Discuss routines: homework, bedtime, playtime, chores
___ Discuss child's feelings, concerns, expectations
___ Take child to school the first day

8. Adopting/Caring for a Pet

Our family has two wonderful cats, Meetz and Muffin. Muffin was adopted from the ASPCA and we followed many of the steps listed below. Meetz, however, walked in our front door one day and decided that our home was his too—he didn't use any list that we know of.

___ Check lease with landlord for pet restrictions
___ Check local ordinances for pet prohibitions
___ Research and read about breeds and their behavior
___ Speak to breeders, pet stores, people who already have same type of pet, veterinarians, local animal shelter
___ Visit pet shows
___ Consider animal with regard to the following:
   a. children
   b. other pets
   c. allergies
   d. amount of attention and care needed
   e. your needs: protection, companionship
   f. your fantasies and fears
___ Consider pros and cons of pet with regard to the following:
   a. size
   b. temperament
   c. food cost
   d. amount of attention and care
   e. life expectancy
   f. exercise
   g. susceptibility to disease
   h. mess factors: shedding, molting, whether pet is housebroken
___ Discuss pet care and expectations with other family members/decide on responsibilities
___ Make final choice

- Buy food, leashes, collars, bowls, tanks, heaters, flea collars, cages, litter box, comb and brush, toys
- Make environment for pet/establish space/put up gates
- Rearrange furniture
- Treat furniture with antipet spray
- Arrange transportation/buy carrying box
- Make final visit to breeders, pet stores, animal shelters/answer advertisements offering pets
- Select/buy/adopt pet
- Pick a name
- Take pet to veterinarian for checkup
- Obtain shots and vaccinations
- Check on diet and vitamins
- Inquire about breeding patterns/spay or neuter
- Get licenses and ID tags
- Buy training manuals
- Contact training schools
- Establish exercise program
- Arrange for backup care when required

9. Buying a New Car

___ Research cars/buy automobile comparison guides
___ Look at new models/ask people who are driving them for their opinions
___ Visit dealer showrooms/read literature on car/ comparison shop
___ Check with friends, the better business bureau about reputation of dealership and automobile considered
___ Make comparison chart of prices, gas mileage, options, negative points
___ Check to see if car will fit into garage
___ Check availability and prices of spare parts
___ Find out extent of servicing network
___ Check to see if any major engineering changes were made in this year's model
___ Test drive
___ Check for leg room, ease of visability, head room, position of rear- and side-view mirrors, seat movement, seat belts, sun visors
___ Decide which options you want
___ Check warranties and guarantees
___ Inquire about availability of weatherproofing and rustproofing/check costs
___ Check on availability of antitheft devices/call insurance company about possible reduction in rates for device
___ Find out price of options and extras
___ Find out cost of insurance
___ Make final decision
___ Negotiate price with dealer
___ Find out waiting period until delivery
___ Shop for financing money: dealer, bank, credit union
___ Arrange financing/fill out forms
___ Sign contracts
___ Compare prices between trade-ins and advertised prices of similar used cars
___ Sell/trade in old car/place ad in newspaper

— Contact insurance company/make changes in coverage/ask to have insurance card mailed immediately
— Check to see if driver's license is valid
— Register/get plates
— Have car inspected
— Arrange for garage space

SEE ALSO:
  CAR CARE (LIST 38)

10. Buying a Used Car

Be cautious when shopping for a used car. Listen carefully for strange noises during the test run. If you're buying on a cold morning, check to see whether the owner has warmed up the car in advance. Be suspicious if he has; it may be a sign that the car doesn't start easily in cold weather. Similarly, if it's a hot day, check the thermostat after driving a while.

___ Decide how much you can spend
___ Decide on year and model of car
___ Research model repair records and reputations of models
___ Answer car ads/visit dealers
___ Test drive car
___ Have car checked by mechanic, consultation service
___ Check body, interior, tires, engine, gas tank (for rust), muffler, shock absorbers, other moving parts
___ Find out about warranties and guarantees (if buying from a dealer)
___ Check to see if warranties and guarantees are transferrable from previous owner
___ Check frequency of repair chart
___ Check book value
___ Check availability of spare parts
___ Find out where you can get car serviced
___ Ask to see car's service record and repair bills
___ Find out type of gas needed and gas mileage
___ Check mileage reading
___ Get estimate for costs of needed repairs
___ Shop for financing: dealer, bank, credit union/make deal/arrange financing/get bill of sale
___ Arrange insurance coverage/have insurance card sent
___ Fill out registration papers
___ Register car/get documents from previous owner
___ Get license plates/install
___ Have car inspected

SEE ALSO: CAR CARE (LIST 38)

11. Lost Wallet/Pocketbook

It's bad enough to lose your wallet or pocketbook without having to face doubts about whether or not you've taken care of everything that needs to be done afterward. Remembering three days later that you have forgotten to stop payment on the checks you lost can be very anxiety provoking.

__ Make complete search of house, office, garage
__ Check pockets of all clothes in house/check laundry
__ Call cleaners
__ Retrace recent routes
__ Call credit-card companies, banks, gas companies, department stores
__ Keep record of date you reported card losses and note name of person to whom you spoke
__ Notify traveler's-check company
__ Place stop orders on remaining checks
__ Stop withdrawals from savings account
__ Replace locks and keys/distribute duplicates to those who had keys
__ Change car lock
__ Make list of everything in wallet or handbag
__ Report loss to police/obtain copy of police report for tax forms and insurance companies
__ Notify insurance company/check cash-loss paragraph in policy
__ Replace bank ID cards
__ Change safety-deposit lock
__ Open new checking and savings accounts
__ Replace check-cashing cards from banks, stores, supermarkets
__ Get/fill out new applications for drivers license and auto registration

_ Get new social security card
_ Notify work place and union/get new ID cards
_ Notify school or college/get new ID cards
_ Replace library card
_ Get applications for special licenses: fishing, hunting
_ Ask organizations to which you belong to send new ID cards: professional organizations, alumni associations
_ Get new voter registration card
_ Contact health organizations and hospitals for new ID cards
_ Visit welfare, Medicaid, Medicare office/get new ID, photo ID
_ Replace food stamp ID
_ Get new medical alert cards
_ Buy new address book
_ Redo list of addresses and phone numbers
_ Redo appointment schedule/fill in new book
_ Replace special papers and receipts
_ Refill prescriptions for drugs you carry in handbag
_ Buy new wallet or handbag
_ Buy new eyeglasses, sunglasses, contact lenses
_ Buy new makeup, comb, brush, pins, barettes, mirror
_ Replace lip balm, hand cream, aspirin, toothpicks, dental floss
_ Buy new pencils, pens, notebooks
_ Replace snapshots

12. Car Accident

It's hoped that you'll never need this list. It is also probable that if you do have to use it you won't have this book with you. We suggest you look over the first part of the list carefully and if you are involved in an accident, we hope you will remember what to do.

We strongly suggest that you not sign any releases, statements, or agreements without consulting your attorney. It is also a good idea to review periodically your insurance policy to make sure that you have adequate coverage.

At the Scene

___ Check to see if anyone is hurt
___ Take note of condition of occupants of other car
___ Call ambulance
___ Call police
___ Obtain other driver's license plate number, name, address, phone number, license number, name of insurance company, name and address on registration
___ Get names, addresses, phone numbers of witnesses
___ Obtain statements from witnesses
___ Get names and badge numbers of police
___ Give police names of witnesses
___ Draw map of accident area / mark where cars started, ended up
___ Write down your version of accident while it's still fresh in your mind
___ Check street lights, traffic lights, signs to see if they are working
___ Arrange towing
___ Remove valuables, papers, CBs, radio, cassette player, portable speaker from car, glove compartment, trunk
___ Remove license plates and valuable car parts

At Home

___ Contact lawyer

___ Make appointment for medical examination

___ Check insurance policy: deductible, towing coverage

___ Obtain estimate on repairs

___ Obtain number of police report

___ Notify insurance company

___ Ask insurance company if car can be repaired before it is inspected

___ Contact mechanic/buy parts/arrange for repairs

___ Take photographs of faulty signs, lights, traffic signals

___ Make record of all expenses: medical bills, towing charges, substitute transportation, loss of salary due to injuries

___ Rent car/set up alternative transportation

___ Arrange time off from work, child care, household help, psychological counseling

13. Complaints

Frustration and anger often rise when we feel victimized by inadequate service, unfair business practices, or the inability to get a replacement for defective merchandise. This list was made for use when you've tried to return an item or make a complaint and you feel unsatisfied with the results.

Repeated phone calls or visits sometime work but often the situation isn't resolved without more drastic actions. This list goes from the most common actions to the more outrageous ones.

___ Withhold outstanding payments
___ Put together receipts, sales slips, bills, canceled checks for proof of purchase
___ Make note of date bought, condition when bought, date broken, circumstances
___ Read warranties, guarantees, contracts
___ Check to see if warranty is from store or from manufacturer
___ Photograph malfunctioning area, part, attachment
___ Decide what you want from store, manufacturer, distributor
___ Decide what you'll settle for
___ Take back item or picture of item to place where purchased/bring sales slip, receipts, warranties, guarantees
___ Speak to supervisor
___ Keep record of all calls: names of people, content of conversations, dates of contact
___ Make copies of all correspondence, bills, receipts
___ Write/call manufacturer/ask for customer relations
___ Work your way up chain of command/call/write president of company
___ Get written repair estimates

__ Make record of all repairs
__ Keep bills and receipts of money spent on problem
__ Research item's performance record
__ Call consumer protection agencies and better business bureau
__ Go to small claims court
__ Write/call government regulatory agencies if utilities are involved
__ Call local newspapers, action groups, media consumer watchdogs
__ Place advertisement in newspaper for people with similar complaints to contact you/organize
__ See attorney
__ Decide whether to file class action suit/sue
__ Make public display: lemons painted on car, picketing, and so forth

14. Establishing/ Re-establishing Credit

Establishing credit is difficult, but re-establishing credit after having received a bad credit rating often seems impossible. We suggest that you not allow your frustrations to get the better of you and that you keep going higher up the executive ladder until at last someone says OK.

The list begins with the common methods of establishing credit and proceeds to tactics you might have to use if you have few assets. If you are trying to re-establish credit, it is important to ascertain why credit is being denied. Sometimes a simple explanation will clear your credit line.

If you feel that credit is being denied because of discriminatory practices, contact a local human rights commission.

Establishing Credit

___ Make list of assets: property, house, car, bank accounts

___ Make list of items which can be used as collateral: jewelry, stocks, antiques, works of art, rare books

___ Obtain letters of financial reference from local merchants, private creditors, banker, investment broker, accountant

___ Apply for major credit cards, charge accounts, bank loans

___ Apply for local credit cards and charge accounts

___ Notify work place that verification of employment will be made

___ Apply for credit from issuers who are going after new business/check advertisements

__ Open checking account with bank that has overdraft
privileges

__ Open savings account

__ Combine small accounts into one large one

__ Apply for gasoline credit cards and check-cashing
cards

__ Apply for small loan/pay back on time

__ Apply for loan at commercial finance company

__ Get cosigner for loans

__ Buy merchandise on installment plans

__ Make sure that your name is on joint credit accounts,
charge accounts, stocks and bonds

__ Consult an accountant

Re-establishing Credit

__ Contact businesses which turned you down/ask for
specific reasons that credit was denied

__ Find out which credit-check company was used

__ Obtain copy of computer printout of your credit report

__ If bad credit is due to error, make sure source of error
supplies correction/get copies of all letters

__ Write explanation of negative credit items for inclusion
on credit report

__ Settle outstanding debts

__ Check legal time limits on reporting negative items

__ Call main office of credit issuer/explain mitigating
circumstances/explain changes in financial situation

__ Refinance outstanding debts/pay them

__ Check with government agencies about rights

__ Call a lawyer

15. Taxes

If you start doing your taxes on April 14, you may not have time to read this list, let alone complete all the items on it. For those who do get an early start, this list covers the two major methods of tackling the task: taking it all to an accountant or doing it yourself.

During the Year

— Keep in mind deductible items: charitable donations, interest on mortgage payment, drug purchases, medical and dental expenses, business expenses, educational expenses, traveling for business
— Pay deductible expenses by check/get receipts
— Keep all checks, receipts
— Keep record of all estimated income tax paid during the year
— Keep record of all nontaxable deposits to bank accounts (gifts)

Two to Three Months before April

— Make appointment with accountant/schedule time to do it yourself
— Discuss with accountant materials and records to be collected
— Check tax literature/buy current tax guides or manuals
— Read instructions in tax booklet
— Get U.S. government publication 17/read for information on deductions and tax benefits
— Review tax forms from previous few years
— Check newspapers, magazines, radio, television, union and trade papers for tax hints
— Talk with colleagues and business associates about their deductions

__ Obtain itemized deduction list from IRS/check for applicability

__ Make list of appropriate areas of deductions/prepare itemized lists of deductions in each area

__ Review diary and other records for business expenses

__ Collect/organize receipts: medical bills, restaurant checks, toll receipts, transportation expenses, educational expenses

__ Arrange receipts in appropriate categories

__ Sort checks/place in appropriate categories

__ List sources of income: salary, capital gains, pensions, rent, royalties, mortgage statements, stocks

__ Arrange W-2 forms, interest statements, dividend slips

__ Deliver checks, figures, receipts, books to accountant

__ Obtain necessary tax forms/get duplicates

__ Sharpen pencils/check batteries in calculator/buy scratch pad

__ Complete forms

__ Call IRS with questions

__ Add and subtract totals twice

__ Get completed forms back from accountant

__ Sign all forms

__ Place social security number on forms and checks

__ Enclose check

__ Duplicate finished forms

__ Put stamps on envelopes/put your return address on the envelopes/mail

16. Separation/Divorce

This list is geared to couples who wish to work out a separation on their own. If at any point you get stuck, you can always seek legal advice, either individually or as a couple.

Should you negotiate the whole process on your own, we suggest that you still consult an attorney at the end to find out about the legal implications of the items you are agreeing to and possibly to have him or her draw up the actual document.

Separation

___ Tell children, family, friends about decision
___ Seek legal advice
___ Make list of property to be divided: money, jewelry, car, house, land, furniture, household items, stocks and bonds
___ Decide who will leave current residence
___ Decide who will take what
___ Discuss finances with accountant (especially if there are substantial assets)
___ Talk to others who have been through process
___ Make list of what you want and bottom limit of what you will accept/decide on areas where you will compromise
___ Seek agreement on the following issues:
    a. property, housing
    b. possessions, income
    c. alimony, maintenance
    d. bank accounts
    e. insurance, inheritance, pensions
    f. legal fees
    g. living apart, mutual releases
    h. cost-of-living increases

    i.   earning differentials and potential
    j.   trust funds
    k.   taxes, deductions
    l.   wills, remarriage
    m. responsibility to other dependents: parents, children, grandparents
    n.   child support
    o.   custody
    p.   child-care schedules
    q.   visitation: holidays, weekends, summer
    r.   residential restrictions
    s.   medical and dental bills
    t.   camps
    u.   schooling, college

- [ ] Consult self-help guides
- [ ] Seek counseling
- [ ] Contact mediation groups / enter arbitration
- [ ] Establish length of time for separation

Divorce

- [ ] Consult with attorney / write divorce agreement on your own
- [ ] Decide grounds for divorce
- [ ] Decide who will get, pay for divorce
- [ ] Check on legality of foreign divorces
- [ ] Compare divorce laws for different states
- [ ] Decide where you will obtain divorce / make necessary arrangements and travel plans

17. Burglary

Unfortunately, it's the rare person these days whose home hasn't been burglarized. If the burglary is on a large scale, don't touch anything until the police have arrived Keeping receipts when you purchase an item is helpful in making insurance claims; in addition, note an item's serial or identification number. Updating your insurance policies periodically will keep you covered for new purchases.

___ Notify police/obtain police report or complaint number
___ Change locks/repair windows/fix doors/check damage for emergency repairs
___ Make careful inventory of what is missing/check the following:
   a. jewelry
   b. stereo, typewriter, cameras, radios, television, taperecorder, videotape recorder, movie projector, furniture
   c. silver
   d. furs, clothing
   e. money, checks, bankbooks, credit cards
   f. keys to apartment, car, safety-deposit box
   g. paintings, antiques, artworks
___ Report theft to local patrol organizations
___ Check/repair alarm system
___ Speak with neighbors/look for possible witnesses
___ Read insurance policy for deductibles, coverage, claim period
___ Decide whether to file claim based on deductible and value of stolen merchandise
___ Notify insurance company/fill out forms
___ Re-analyze security system/update
___ Take pictures of any damage to house or apartment
___ Straighten house

___ Organize receipts for missing items
___ Organize bills for repairs on apartment, house, appliances, car
___ Visit local pawnshops, antique stores, jewelry stores to look for your property
___ Replace needed items

18. Serious Illness/ Hospital Stay

Many items on this list suggest that you discuss issues with your doctor, family, or others. In our years of working with patients and families we've found that many people are intimidated about asking questions or sharing fears. Adjustment to illness, however, is often easier when people can make informed decisions. Most physicians are willing to talk with you honestly if you let them know that you want them to. Some suggestions on the list refer to patients, others to family members.

Planned Hospitalization

__ Check medical and hospital coverage
__ Contact AMA for referrals/contact teaching hospital for names of leading people in field
__ Get second opinion
__ Read about disease
__ Contact organizations that deal with specific illness
__ Notify employer and colleagues
__ Ask doctor for options
__ Ask doctor for explanation of unfamiliar medical terms
__ Discuss procedure, incision site with doctor, surgeon
__ Rearrange home routines/arrange babysitting and house sitting
__ Talk to children about plans
__ Check on hospital regulations, services, visiting hours
__ Check with hospital personnel about overnight visiting regulations for relatives
__ Leave medications at home/take a list of medications currently taken

__ Leave valuables and jewelry at home
__ Pack bag/prepare clothes you'll need for trip home.
__ Buy books, magazines, games
__ Take medical insurance cards and suitcase
__ Arrange transportation to hospital

Hospital Procedures

__ Arrange for television/phone
__ Discuss need for private nurses with doctor/arrange for private nurses
__ Get telephone numbers: ward phone, doctors, nurses' station, phone in closest lounge
__ Contact clergyman
__ Arrange for friends to wait with family during surgery
__ Ask doctor for diagnosis, prognosis, course of treatment
__ Ask doctor to explain surgery
__ Discuss need for second opinion with family and physician
__ Ask doctor for explanations of all procedures
__ Ask doctor about type of incision
__ See social worker about discharge planning and counseling
__ Talk with friends or counselor about reactions to illness and loss of physical abilities
__ Discuss/decide changes in role with family
__ Discuss/decide changes in career and business
__ Discuss/decide changes in diet, activities, routines
__ Apply for disability, sick leave, compensation (this may have to be done before you enter hospital)
__ File medical insurance forms
__ Contact support groups
__ Discuss hospices, nursing home, alternative care if unable to return home
__ Check/arrange for stay in rehabilitation center
__ Check on home care, nurses, equipment for return home.
__ Arrange for help at home
__ Rent/arrange equipment: hospital bed, oxygen, crutches, walker, wheelchair, braces

___ Arrange transportation for leaving hospital

Terminal Illness

___ Prepare will
___ Withdraw money from joint accounts
___ Delegate power of attorney
___ Check safety-deposit box
___ Discuss with family your decisions about life-support systems, funeral arrangements, financial matters
___ Discuss with doctor and family how far to carry out extraordinary medical procedures
___ Contact clergyman
___ Arrange coverage for bedside vigil
___ Talk with social worker, counselor to help patient and family deal with emotional aspects of illness

SEE ALSO:

DEATH/FUNERAL ARRANGEMENTS (LIST 19)
BEFORE YOU GO (LIST 40)
PACKING FOR A HOSPITAL STAY (LIST 68)

19. Death/Funeral Arrangements

When someone dies we are faced with enormous pain and loss as well as the strain of managing funeral arrangements. We suggest you ask family and friends to share the tasks with you.

Preparations

___ Join burial society or prepaid mortuary plan/check on death benefits through union or fraternal organization

___ Make will/have will witnessed

___ Prepare and organize documents outlining your estate

___ Appoint executor

___ Delegate power of attorney

___ Plan/write out funeral plans with regard to burial, cremation, type of service, music, flowers, where to send donations instead of flowers

___ Discuss "living will" (how far to carry extraordinary life-saving measures) with doctor and attorney

___ Set up trust fund/consult tax attorney

___ Decide who gets sentimental gifts, endowments, money

___ Purchase cemetary plot

___ Select undertaker

___ Buy casket

___ Arrange funeral service

___ Buy space in columbarium

___ Arrange to leave body to a medical school/fill out forms

___ Arrange to donate body organs: corneas, kidneys, heart, skin

___ Sign uniform donor card/tell family, friends, or lawyer your intentions

— Tell lawyer, family, friends about important unknown facts: previous marriage, other children, or treatment for mental disorder (in case will is contested)
— Tell lawyer, executor, family about bills you have been paying in secret: medical expenses for sick relative, support for lover or unknown child
— Check beneficiaries listed on all insurance policies
— Give someone a key to safety-deposit box
— Make list of all banks, safety-deposit boxes, insurance policies, stocks, deeds to property, credit unions, debts
— Make list of personal information: parents' birthdays and places of birth, membership in fraternal organizations, schools attended, service record, serial numbers, social security number, facts for obituary
— Leave plans with lawyer, family, friends

Immediately After the Death

— Get at least 10 copies of the death certificate
— Call personal doctor if you have medical condition that might worsen under stress
— Notify medical authorities if deceased signed uniform donor card
— Call relatives or friends to stay with you
— Secure home of deceased/remove small valuables
— Contact embassy or consulate if abroad

Funeral Arrangements

— Check to see if deceased left instructions about funeral arrangements/check for deeds to cemetary plot
— Ask friends, clergy, union to recommend funeral home
— Select funeral director and mortuary
— Check to see if deceased had prepaid mortuary plan and burial plot/contact union, fraternal organizations, armed forces for possible benefits
— Decide about autopsy
— Choose medical school for donation of body/fill out forms
— Call medical school if deceased prearranged donation
— Call friend or relative to go with you to funeral home

___ Call memorial societies for help in determining type and cost of funeral service
___ Decide on price limit for funeral
___ Ask for itemized breakdown of all costs
___ Decide whether to bury, cremate, embalm, entomb
___ Discuss desires with funeral home
___ Choose/buy casket, crypt, urn, grave liner
___ Buy cemetary plot/buy place in columbarium
___ Check with cemetary to see if vault is required
___ Choose gravestone or marker
___ Decide on open or closed coffin
___ Decide time and place of service
___ Arrange transportation to cemetary, funeral
___ Call clergyman/plan service: military, fraternal, religious, memorial, family, written
___ Reserve chapel
___ Check on family traditions, religious customs
___ Choose people to give eulogy/choose readings
___ Appoint pallbearers
___ Bring burial clothes to funeral home
___ Decide on flowers/buy family spray/decide what to do with flowers after the funeral
___ Choose music
___ Arrange for flag to be placed over casket
___ Notify family, friends, business associates, fraternal organizations/check deceased's phone book for names
___ Write announcement/notify newspapers/write obituary
___ Decide where you would like donations to be sent: favorite charity, hospital, alma mater
___ Make arrangements for out-of-town guests
___ Arrange babysitting
___ Hire help: house cleaning, catering
___ Ask friends for help with specific tasks: meals, babysitting, cleaning, phone answering
___ Plan after-funeral meal, drinks, mourning period, where you'll be receiving people
___ Make list of callers and guests
___ Write thank-you notes for flowers, for visits, to pallbearers, for mass and sympathy cards

Legal Arrangements

— Notify deceased's landlord/arrange for repayment of security
— Stop deliveries: newspaper, milk
— Arrange to forward mail
— Stop utilities/arrange for repayment of deposits
— Collect important documents: insurance policies, bankbooks, safety-deposit keys, stock certificates, property deeds
— Notify lawyer/have will read
— Call deceased's accountant, stockbroker, insurance agent
— Check laws pertaining to access to safety-deposit box, bank accounts
— Make many copies of death certificate, marriage licenses, divorce papers, discharge papers, tax forms, W-2 forms, bills from funeral home, disability certification
— Settle medical payments
— Check with employer for accrued wages, vacation pay, severance pay, death benefits, pension fund
— Notify union/check death benefits
— Call workmen's compensation board if death was work related
— Notify social security office/fill out forms
— Notify other government programs if person not covered by social security
— Notify Veterans Administration
— Check all fraternal organizations, schools, professional organizations for possible benefits
— Check death benefits from states in which no-fault insurance laws are in effect if death occurred in automobile accident
— Look over insurance policies for names of beneficiaries, type of benefits, how benefits are paid
— Apply for loans needed immediately: tuition, home repairs, mortgage payment
— Pay outstanding bills
— Go through clothing/dispose of personal effects
— Look through papers and books

__ Check for pawn tickets, public locker keys, dry-cleaning tickets, lottery tickets, IOUs

__ File small-estate affidavit/check with lawyer

__ Contact executor of will

If You Are Executor

__ File for probate

__ Notify beneficiaries of benefits due them

__ Get appraisal of items in estate

__ Prepare inventory of all items in estate

__ Publish notice for creditors to come forth with bills

__ Notify debtors that debts are due

20. Safeguards against Fire

___ Buy fire extinguishers/install in key places: kitchen, workshop, laundry room, near boiler or furnace, teach family how to use/check for recharging
___ Install smoke detectors/check periodically
___ Buy fire ladders
___ Plan fire escape routes/practice fire drills with family
___ Post fire department number near all phones
___ Leave keys near gates, hatches, doors on escape route
___ Check house for fire hazards: curtains near stove and fireplace, improper ventilation, grease buildup on stove, flammable goods, papers near appliances
___ Clean out fire hazards from house: oily rags, papers, boxes of old clothes and books
___ Check wiring and electrical cords for fraying/replace or repair
___ Check plugs and outlets for overloading
___ Install safety cutout switches on furnaces
___ Have fuel tanks and lines inspected for damage, leakage
___ Buy adequate fire insurance
___ Keep a first-aid burn kit in house
___ Post locations of nearest fire-alarm boxes
___ Have chimney cleaned regularly
___ Use fireplace screen
___ Keep rugs away from front of fireplace
___ Install a hearth on wooden floor in front of fireplace
___ Check space heaters
___ Keep back of television, refrigerator, and other heat-generating appliances well ventilated
___ Keep salt, baking soda near stove for grease fire
___ Keep Christmas trees and other flammable materials away from radiators and heaters
___ Install lightning rods on house, garage, garden shed

21. Safeguards against Theft

___ Engrave social security numbers onto major appliances: stereo, television, radio, tape recorder, typewriter
___ File list of valuables and their identification numbers with police/file copy with your personal papers
___ Rent safety-deposit box/store valuables
___ Buy theft insurance/update periodically to include cost of new valuables
___ Make security check on house and car/upgrade locks, alarms, gates, window bars
___ Set up automatic light timer
___ Install hood lock, trunk-lock shield, cutout switch on car
___ Drill holes in window frames/put nails in holes
___ Keep light timer on
___ Keep radio on when gone
___ Instruct children about whom to let into house
___ Separate money from credit cards/sew Velcro to wallet and inside coat pocket
___ Get traveler's checks
___ Wear money belt when traveling
___ Keep pocketbook closed

22. Finding an Apartment

This list is meant to reflect the differences in availability of apartments throughout the country. In a tight market, it's important to follow through on leads immediately.

The beginning of the list contains the commonplace methods of finding an apartment and the end of the list includes some more unconventional ideas. Avoid buying lists from agents because these lists are often obsolete by the time you get them.

___ Review finances/decide on price range/fix outer limit for rent

___ Analyze/make list of desired features: number of rooms, fireplaces, view, noise potential, nearness to workplace, shopping, transportation

___ Make list of your minimum requirements

___ Decide if you want or need lease

___ Research desired locales/make priority list

___ Decide if you want a roommate

___ Arrange 24-hour phone accessibility via answering machine, answering service

___ Arrange to have cash or check available for deposit

___ Ask a friend or family member to accompany you if you need help making a decision

___ Check eligibility for special housing: artists, elderly, handicapped, professional, minority, low income

___ Tell friends, family, shopkeepers, colleagues, previous landlords—everyone—that you are looking

___ Check on reputation of real estate agents

___ Register with real estate agents/check on fees/call frequently

___ Ask if agent has seen apartment/ask for description before going to see apartment

___ Ask if apartment is rent stabilized or controlled

___ Find out the hour of first newspaper edition/buy early
___ Check newspaper ads in many papers
___ Check neighborhood newspaper ads
___ Spend time in neighborhood/talk with local residents/ ask people you meet if they know of apartments
___ Check local bulletin boards in bookstores, colleges, schools, hospitals
___ Ask local church and community centers for access to bulletin boards and newspapers
___ Go door to door/look for empty apartments and moving vans/ask superintendents and doormen
___ Check company newspapers for transfers/contact the people who are moving and ask for the name of their landlord
___ Read about housing being built
___ Put name on waiting lists with agents for desired buildings and buildings under construction
___ Check in neighborhoods that are being renovated
___ Check recently registered deeds at courthouse/
___ Offer a reward for a new apartment/post notices in area where you want to live
___ Check neighborhoods for apartment furniture sales/ ask sellers if they are moving
___ Read obituaries for recent vacancies

23. Moving

We've included items that refer to both styles of moving: doing it yourself and hiring a mover. Choose the ones that apply to your situation.

Some items do not apply if you're moving far from your previous residence; if that's the case, just add them to Establishing Yourself in a New Neighborhood (list 24). Other items apply only to long-distance moves.

Six to Eight Weeks Before

__ Plan/arrange farewell party
__ Notify relatives and friends of plans
__ Arrange moving date
__ Notify subscriptions, charge accounts, insurance companies, friends, relatives, motor vehicle office, banks of new address
__ Notify post office of new address/have mail forwarded
__ Notify school and business of plans to move
__ Make hotel reservations
__ Order new furniture and appliances/arrange delivery to new home
__ Notify old landlord/arrange for security reimbursement
__ Arrange use of elevator on moving day
__ Hire mover/read contract and insurance provisions (especially for long-distance movers)/get written estimates
__ Establish delivery date for long-distance moving
__ Decide if you want mover to pack/arrange
__ Ask mover how payment is to be made
__ Rent truck/ask friends to help
__ Get packing crates, bins, boxes, wardrobes from mover
__ Get cartons
__ Buy sealing tape
__ Save newspapers for wrapping
__ Discard/sell unwanted items

One Month Before

___ Pack items that won't be needed immediately
___ Tape screws to objects they belong to
___ Label cartons as to contents and where they go in new house
___ Make inventory lists of cartons that you don't plan to unpack immediately
___ Arrange for child care and pet care on moving day
___ Arrange time off from work for moving, waiting for utility installation, deliveries

Two Weeks Before

___ Confirm reservation with mover, hotel, delivery people
___ Get cleaning and laundry from shops
___ Return library books
___ Settle bills with local merchants/close local charge accounts
___ Get back tools and equipment lent to neighbors
___ Return all borrowed items
___ Call workmen to arrange date for appliances to be disconnected

One Week Before

___ Arrange date for connection of appliances at new residence
___ Arrange date for phone and utilities to be cut off at old residence
___ Arrange date for phone and utilities to be connected at new residence
___ Arrange to have phone calls forwarded to new number
___ Give phone company new address
___ Arrange fuel delivery at new residence
___ Arrange fuel delivery to be stopped at old residence/ assess amount of fuel left for closing purposes
___ Arrange for electricity and gas to be turned off/give new address to utility company
___ Stop services/arrange for services at new residence: gardening, garbage pickup, soda, newspaper, milk delivery
___ Cancel memberships in local clubs and religious institutions

___ Remove air conditioners, built-in items, television antennas

___ Remove pictures and fixtures/tape screws and picture hooks to objects

___ Repair/restore walls to original condition

___ Check on operating instructions for new home from previous tenant or owner

___ Get keys to new residence

___ Plan menu for first meals in new place/take food with you

___ Take lightbulbs, toilet paper, cleaning supplies, trash bags, and other basic goods to new residence

___ Pack items, clothing, bedding, kitchen utensils needed for first few days/take to new house

___ Clean new residence

___ Close bank accounts/transfer funds

___ Arrange to leave keys to old residence

___ Inform police and neighbors if house is to be empty/ leave lights on

___ Say good-byes

Moving Day

___ Pack/move heirlooms, valuables, plants, separately with special care

___ Check attic, cellar, closets, garage, yard, hamper, clothesline, garden shed for leftover items

___ Have cash on hand to tip movers

___ Pack remaining items

___ Tape drawers closed

___ Clean old place/defrost refrigerator/disconnect/leave refrigerator open

___ Turn down thermostat

___ Lock house

SEE ALSO:

   FINDING A ROOMMATE/MOVING IN WITH SOMEONE (LIST 1)
   ESTABLISHING YOURSELF IN A NEW NEIGHBORHOOD
      (LIST 24)   BUYING A HOUSE (LIST 25)

24. Establishing Yourself in a New Neighborhood

___ Introduce yourself and family to neighbors
___ Take walk/get map/drive through neighborhood
___ Check on local transportation, routes, stops
___ Find out emergency numbers, location of fire-alarm boxes, hospitals, police station
___ Open new bank account
___ Introduce yourself and family to local merchants
___ Open charge accounts in local stores
___ Fill out check-cashing applications at stores
___ Arrange deliveries: newspapers, food, mail, milk
___ Arrange garbage pickup
___ Give friends new address and phone number
___ Introduce yourself to postal workers
___ Enroll children in school/transfer records
___ Change address on license, charge accounts, credit cards, car registration, medical insurance card
___ Find new doctor, dentist, mechanic, veterinarian/ transfer records
___ Visit/join local organizations, religious groups, neighborhood associations, scout troops
___ Buy local newspaper/check bulletin boards for events
___ Find babysitters
___ Visit library/apply for new card
___ Change voting registration
___ Plan/arrange housewarming
___ Leave a set of extra house and car keys with neighbor

SEE ALSO:
  RENOVATING (LIST 29)

25. Buying a House

Buying a house is an emotional as well as a financial investment, so be careful. Those tempting details like working fireplaces and stately trees, which have you reaching for your pen, need to be balanced against the uninsulated roof and the sagging front porch.

___ Choose a neighborhood
___ Speak to banker and accountant/ask how much you can afford based on your income/ask about tax breaks
___ Decide on price range based on maximum net monthly carrying costs
___ Make list of essential features: style of house, number of rooms, acreage, fireplace, garage, basement, attic, nearness to schools, shopping, public transportation, work place
___ Make list of minimum features you will accept
___ Check on commuting time and traffic
___ Register with agents and check newspapers
___ Ask for description of house before viewing it
___ View house
___ Walk around property
___ Determine upkeep of grounds, landscaping chores/ determine degree of sun and shade
___ Check zoning regulations, building codes, long-range plans for area
___ Find out local restrictions on building occupancy, renovations
___ Check certificate of occupancy and rent controls for building
___ Check operating costs: fuel, utilities, mortgage
___ Check upkeep costs: painting, repairs, blacktopping driveway, cleaning septic tank, trimming hedges
___ Get bills from current owner
___ Get tax bills: school, sewer, water, assessments

___ Find out what goes with house: gardening equipment, fixtures, kitchen and laundry appliances/make agreement

___ Have building and land inspected by engineer, architect, building inspection service, or other experts/ check the following:

   a. insulation values in roof and walls

   b. orientation of house to sun

   c. construction materials

   d. flow rate, purity of water supply

   e. site drainage, type of soil, stability of house site and foundation, basement

   f. heating system, electrical system, plumbing, roof, septic tank, sewers, well

   g. leaks, flooding

   h. termites, rodents, other pests

   i. rot, mildew, recent repairs

   j. fireplaces, chimneys

   k. windows, doors, storms, screens, frames

___ Determine if particular heating system will worsen medical problems: asthma, skin problems, rheumatism

___ Find out when house will be vacated

___ Estimate major expenses: attaching to sewer lines, extra phone lines

___ Check on garbage pickup services, location of town dump, permits

___ Estimate upkeep needs: snow shoveling, lawn mowing

___ Assess how present furnishings will fit into new house

___ Measure garage space/check local parking restrictions

___ Check access to shopping

___ Check local public transportation

___ Walk neighborhood/visit neighbors/discover peer groups for adults and children

___ Research quality of local schools/ask neighbors

___ Ask local residents about seasonal problems: mosquitos, flooding, strong winds

___ Buy topographic map

___ Check if house is in a flood hazard zone, fault zone

___ Consider how site will look in different seasons

___ Check feasibility of desired renovations with architect and local zoning officials

— Get estimate on renovations, repairs
— Determine if you can afford house, renovations, taxes
— Review costs with accountant
— Ask broker for recommendations: lenders, title company, inspectors/ask for specific reasons people are being recommended
— Decide who pays for required inspections
— Hire attorney/ask about fees
— Check deed for restrictions, easements
— Set contract date/go to contract
— Comparison shop on financing/apply for mortgage/ask about owner financing
— Check on home-improvement loans
— Get mortgage confirmation/send lawyer's name and address on commitment letter to bank
— Set closing date/tell bank
— Discuss with lawyer whether house will be vacant during interim/take appropriate measures to safeguard it
— Have title searched/buy title insurance
— Buy needed insurance: fire, life, flood, liability, theft
— Have property surveyed
— Coordinate dates of moving from current housing to new house
— Set moving date
— Notify utilities to turn on service
— Make list of immediate repairs, renovations/arrange schedules with repair people
— Make list of long-term repairs, renovations
— Make list of appliances needed
— Order appliances, new furniture, screens, storm doors and windows, awnings
— Ask attorney about money or certified checks needed for closing/check that all monies deposited to your account have cleared
— Get money
— Assess amount of fuel left/arrange delivery
— Read over contract before signing
— Close deal

SEE ALSO: MOVING (LIST 23)   ESTABLISHING YOURSELF IN A NEW NEIGHBORHOOD (LIST 24)   BUYING LAND (LIST 26) APPLYING FOR MORTGAGE (LIST 28) RENOVATING (LIST 29)

26. Buying Land

A magnificent view in winter may disappear as the leaves come out in spring. Half your property may become inaccessible after the first snow. Obviously, you can't wait through all the seasons before buying, but we suggest you do some research to ensure you'll get the most pleasure from your purchase.

__ Choose the area you will look in/decide how far away is acceptable

__ Drive through area to see general economic condition, esthetic qualities, nearness to emergency services, shopping, banks, recreation

__ Drive through area at different times of day/check traffic flow

__ Check local zoning ordinances for minimal acreage needed to build, water system, septic system, type of house allowed

__ Make list of qualities you want on land: stream, woods, view

__ Contact land agents and real estate agents

__ Read newspaper ads/ask local people who is selling land

__ Walk land

__ Check deed for restrictions

__ Buy/study topographic maps of area

__ Get estimates for putting in access road

__ Check deed for easements

__ Get estimates on putting in electricity, phone, other utilities

__ Call expert for estimate on well/check existing wells and springs

__ Ask neighbors how far down they found water

__ Check cement seal and casing on existing well

__ Check water rights

__ See if water supply goes dry in summer

__ Have water tested/check for pollution

__ Have percolation test

__ Have site inspected for ground stability

- Check type of vegetation/check for erosion
- Estimate ease of removal of vegetation and boulders
- Check type of soil on property for farming, gardening, drainage
- Find out who maintains access roads
- Check on land taxes, county assessments, school tax
- Check future building projects in area: shopping center, dam, highway, housing
- Discover seasonal problems: floods, wildlife, pests
- Look at land and view in winter to see what was hidden by foliage
- Check seasonal changes in neighborhoods: summer camps, ski lodge, local or regional fairs and festivals, tourist trade
- Inspect bridges and roads for load-bearing capacity, deterioration
- Find out local services: recreation, swimming, garbage removal, schools, snowplowing
- Check access to public transportation
- Compare costs to similar property elsewhere
- Find out who owns timber, hunting, mineral rights
- Visit neighbors
- Spend full day on property/check where sunlight falls at different times of day
- Consult engineers, architect about building site
- Check on local costs for building house
- Figure degree of slope on building site
- Hire lawyer
- Arrange contract and closing date
- Check for liens against property
- Search title
- Get survey estimates/have survey taken
- Arrange financing
- Buy insurance: liability, flood, fire, theft
- Close deal
- Get signs made: name, No Trespassing, Fishing OK
- Register/post land usage
- Coordinate building site with septic system, well, view, sunlight, shade, direction of wind
- Plan home/get estimates

27. Buying a Co-op

This section is divided into two separate lists: the first is for those people who live in a building that is about to go co-op; the second is for those who are buying into a new or converted building that is offering cooperative apartments, or for those who are buying into a preexisting cooperative apartment arrangement.

For all situations, an attorney who specializes in cooperative deals and who knows state law on cooperatives is often essential in helping you to understand the prospectus, and then to negotiate the deal.

If Your Building Is Going Co-op

__ Read owner's proposal for conversion
__ Check whether plan is eviction or noneviction
__ Poll tenants for their reactions
__ Form tenants' group
__ Hire co-op lawyer
__ Research tenants' rights: for elderly tenants, percentage needed to convert, deadlines for decisions
__ Choose leadership for tenants' group/form committees
__ Decide whether to sign "no buy" pledge
__ Document tenants' problems with apartments/figure replacements costs of appliances
__ Hire engineer to prepare report on building/outline problems
__ Get estimates on repairs
__ Hire accountant to explain owners' figures
__ Decide if you want apartment as home or investment
__ Consider necessary renovations to apartment/get estimates
__ Call your accountant to determine your price range/ consider the following:
  a. tax breaks
  b. carrying charges
  c. cash on hand

    d. interest lost on money used for down payment
    e. loans
    f. interest rates and term
    g. expected increase in taxes, co-op loan, repairs
    h. cost of renovations on your apartment

— Compare net costs with renting similar apartment or with buying other co-ops

— Work in tenants' group to redefine offer to your advantage

— Negotiate on the following:
    a. increased reserve fund for repairs
    b. lowering interest on co-op loan
    c. increasing term of co-op loan
    d. lowering asking price
    e. state of building when delivered
    f. costs of major renovations to building

— Read through state-approved prospectus

— Go over prospectus with attorney and accountant

— Negotiate further changes with landlord

— Make decision whether to accept or reject prospectus

— Make individual decision to buy

— Check that subscription agreement is dependent on getting financing (in order to get deposit back)

— Put down deposit

— Check owner financing

— Check if owner has gotten bulk co-op loan agreement from bank

— Research which banks give co-op loans

— Work out carrying costs based on different co-op loan plans: larger down payment, longer terms

— Check other sources for financing: families, insurance policies, credit union

— Go to contract

— Search for liens against building and sponsor/make closing dependent on search

— Buy needed insurance

— Set closing date/talk over with lawyer consequences of closing at a date after title is handed over to tenants' group

— Ask attorney about monies needed for closing/check that monies deposited into account have cleared

__ Close
__ Get home improvement loan
__ Prepare for renovations

Buying into a Co-op

__ Call accountant to determine general price range you can afford/consider the following:
   a. tax breaks
   b. cash on hand
   c. loans
   d. interest on loans
   e. assets
   f. expenses
__ Make list of essential features: fireplace, garage, view, terrace, air conditioning, desired floor, number of rooms
__ Make list of minimum features you will accept
__ Check on commuting time and traffic
__ Register with agents and check newspaper
__ Check zoning regulations, long-range plans for area
__ Check access to shopping, public transportation, services
__ Research quality of local schools
__ Walk neighborhood/discover peer groups for children and adults
__ Ask local residents about seasonal problems: mosquitos, flooding
__ Ask agents for description of co-op before viewing
__ View co-ops
__ Assess how present furnishings will fit in
__ Decide if you are interested in purchasing co-op

Buying a Cooperative in Converted or New Building

__ Get prospectus
__ Hire attorney who specializes in co-ops/ask fees
__ Go over prospectus with attorney
__ Determine financial and physical status of building/hire building inspector to check heating, plumbing, electrical systems

___ Inquire about reserve fund
___ Check feasibility of desired renovations with architect, engineer
___ Get estimates on renovations, repairs
___ Find out if sponsor is offering financing/find out terms
___ See accountant/consider actual costs and affordability based on prospectus, maintenance figures, renovation costs, income, mortgage payments
___ Discuss with sponsor price, changes desired in apartment, condition of building
___ Go to contract
___ Comparison shop on financing/decide about sponsor financing/apply for co-op loan
___ Check on renovation loans
___ Get co-op loan confirmation/discuss with attorney
___ Set closing date/discuss with attorney consequences of closing at a time later than the date on which title is handed over to tenants' group
___ Obtain title report and search liens against sponsor if closing on building coincides with your closing
___ Obtain abstract report on tenants' corporation and search for liens against sponsor if closing at later date than building closing
___ Decide on moving date/find out when apartment will be ready and when you have to vacate your present premises
___ Buy needed insurance
___ Notify utilities to turn on service
___ Order appliances and furniture if needed
___ Make list of immediate repairs and renovations/ arrange
___ Ask attorney about money or certified checks needed for closing/check that all monies deposited into your account have cleared
___ Get money
___ Close deal

Buying into Existing Co-op

___ Ask price
___ Hire attorney who specializes in co-ops/ask fees
___ Negotiate price with owner/ask about what items will be included in apartment

___ Get copy of lease from owner
___ Have attorney review existing co-op loan from tenants' corporation
___ Find out from tenants' corporation about needed repairs, operating budget/find out about reserve fund
___ Hire building inspector or engineer to inspect building and apartment
___ Check feasibility of desired renovations with architect, engineer
___ Get estimates on renovations, repairs
___ See accountant/consider actual costs and affordability based on income, maintenance, loans, renovation costs, mortgage payments
___ Go to contract
___ Submit necessary financial statements, references to tenants' association or board of directors/find out if you are approved to join co-op
___ Comparison shop on financing/apply for co-op loan
___ Check on renovation loans
___ Get co-op loan confirmation/discuss with attorney
___ Get abstract on tenants' corporation
___ Search for liens against owner of co-op apartment you are buying
___ Set closing date
___ Decide on moving date/find out when apartment will be vacated and coordinate with time of leaving your present premises
___ Buy needed insurance
___ Notify utilities to transfer service
___ Order appliances and furniture
___ Make list of immediate repairs and renovations/ arrange
___ Ask attorney about money or certified checks for closing/check that all monies deposited into your account have cleared
___ Get money
___ Close deal

28. Applying for a Mortgage

There are two basic rules to follow when applying for a mortgage. The first is to work out in detail your financial ability to carry your monthly expenses including the proposed mortgage. In order to do so you have to follow the second rule, namely to bring in as many documents as you can to prove your case.

___ Assess cash resources
___ Make list of assets and liabilities
___ Estimate financial obligations and income through next five years, allowing for inflation
___ Make list of monthly debts
___ Figure outside limits of what you can pay per month
___ Buy interest and payback book/estimate down payment and figure monthly charges for term desired
___ Make list of collateral
___ Obtain copy of personal credit report/set up personal credit: take out small loan, pay installment debts on time
___ Put together numbers and locations of your savings and checking accounts/indicate same for any closed accounts in same bank
___ Collect latest pay stub, income tax statements, written verification of employment
___ Notify credit references that they may be contacted
___ Ask family for private mortgage loan
___ Discuss possible owner-granted mortgage
___ Discuss taking over mortgage from original owner
___ Check into private mortgage lending firms or people
___ Check eligibility for special mortgages: FHA, credit unions, unions, Veterans Administration
___ Ask real estate broker to check around for mortgages
___ Find out which banks in area are granting mortgages
___ Make appointment with loan officer/get explanation of costs/have bank send you written mortgage policy

___ Compare rates/figure our percentages based on all costs, including fees

___ Check on bank requirements and rules: termite inspection, life insurance

___ Arrange to have appraiser come to see house/talk to neighbors and get idea of how much they paid/get independent appraisal

___ Check whether bank refunds origination fee if they stop the process

___ Check bank regulations to see if you qualify as a preferred customer and have points taken off the mortgage rate

___ Check to see if lender requires a reserve account

___ Open accounts in bank that may grant mortgage

___ Make list of bank officers who work in bank

___ Decide whether to get fixed or variable rate

___ Fill out application/mail/drop off in person

___ Get name of loan officer whom you can call

___ Arrange to put money into reserve fund

___ Get monies for lawyer, fees

___ Hire lawyer/go over contracts and terms

___ Buy needed insurance: fire, hazard, mortgage, liability

___ Check bank's notification schedule/call if you haven't heard from them

___ Make copies of all documents submitted to bank

For Co-op

___ Pick applicable items from above

___ Check to see if your building comes under a specific bank's bulk commitment for financing

___ Check bank for listing of co-ops they are financing

___ Bring in subscription agreement if new conversion

___ Bring in contract of sale if co-op is a resale

___ Bring in ID if you have no accounts with bank

SEE ALSO:
    BUYING A HOUSE (LIST 25)   BUYING A CO-OP (LIST 27)

29. Renovating

This list covers various options: renovating yourself, hiring an architect and contractor, and hiring individual craftspeople whom you supervise.

The first phase is creating your dreams. The second phase is finding out from experts if your dreams are realistic. The third phase is finding out the cost of your dreams. The final phase is hiring others to create your dreams or doing the work yourself.

___ Decide on changes wanted
___ Make list of specific jobs
___ Decide which jobs take priority
___ Decide what you will do yourself
___ Decide what you will have professionals do
___ Buy "how to" books/learn skills
___ Buy needed tools
___ Buy safety equipment: masks, goggles, hard hat, gloves
___ Order special equipment and appliances that may take time to get delivered
___ Consult specialists in renovation: brownstone societies, restoration groups, historical societies, preservationists
___ Consult others who have done renovations
___ Hire expediter, architect, engineer who is expert on building codes and regulations/have them do the following:
   a. check local building codes
   b. check energy-saving regulations
   c. check deed restrictions and water rights
   d. check property lines if you plan to build extension
   e. determine which walls are load bearing
   f. check certificate of occupancy
   g. apply for new certificate of occupancy/file prospective changes

h. file for building permits
i. submit plans to regulatory organizations: selectmen, town council, zoning board

___ Consult with architect or designer
___ Make floor plan/build models
___ Set budget
___ Apply for home improvement loans
___ Get money to pay workers, suppliers, delivery men
___ Let neighbors know you are renovating
___ Consult with friends, better business bureau for names of reputable workers
___ Get several estimates
___ Make final decision about work to be done by others
___ Hire contractor, plumber, electrician, painter, carpenter, mason, glazer
___ Get contracts from workers/get written price
___ Establish date work is to begin and estimated length of job
___ Order plumbing, electrical, hardware fixtures, supplies, paint, wallpaper
___ Rent equipment
___ Coordinate tasks
___ Arrange necessary child care
___ Arrange for care of pets and plants
___ Arrange to eat and sleep elsewhere
___ Prepare/freeze meals ahead of time
___ Protect rugs and floors
___ Cover/protect furniture and valuables
___ Seal cabinets, closets, rooms with plastic during messy jobs: floor scraping, demolition, plastering
___ Stock drinks and coffee for workers
___ Have extra keys made for workers
___ Withhold final payment until job is completed
___ Make work schedule for yourself
___ Ask others to help
___ Establish credit at supply stores
___ Arrange deliveries and person to accept deliveries
___ Let sanitation workers know you are renovating
___ Arrange removal of debris/hire dumpster
___ Consult decorator
___ Buy/order furnishings

30. Finding a Job

Following up leads, answering advertisements immediately, and aggressively contacting places for interviews are helpful not only in landing a job but also in creating a positive feeling about oneself. When unemployment is high, you may have to be more creative in your tactics, as the last few items on the list suggest.

___ Consult résumé books/write résumé/type
___ Notify references that they may be contacted
___ Compose cover letter for résumé
___ Buy stationery, envelopes, stamps
___ Make list of skills
___ Decide which jobs you would prefer and which jobs you would settle for
___ Decide on salary requirements
___ Make list of dates of past employment, names and addresses of references, schools, previous employers for applications and interviews
___ Make list of questions you want to ask: benefits, hours, salary, overtime
___ Practice interviewing
___ Plan route if you have several interviews scheduled
___ Select wardrobe for interviews/clean clothes and shoes
___ Buy newspapers/check want ads
___ Make list of places you have called/note responses
___ Register at employment agencies/ask about fees
___ Ask for leads from friends, colleagues, relatives
___ Call contacts in your field
___ Call employers and businesses that interest you/send résumés
___ Contact personnel departments/get name of personnel director

___ Ask places that don't have jobs if they know who is hiring
___ Check with past employers
___ Contact government agencies: state unemployment services, CETA offices
___ Contact unions
___ Contact training programs
___ See professional and trade bulletins and newspapers
___ Consult professional societies and associations
___ Call college placement services
___ Check bulletin boards in places you want to work
___ Contact organizations and unions to find out when exams or hiring are to take place
___ Sign up for qualifying exams
___ Take courses to help in passing qualifying exams
___ Contact temporary agencies (temporary jobs can become permanent)
___ Go door to door/apply in person
___ Look for businesses and shops that are opening
___ Volunteer to work at place you want
___ Place want ad about yourself in newspaper

SEE ALSO:
STARTING A JOB (LIST 31)

31. Starting a Job

Preparations

— Find out about uniforms, dress codes
— Clean/iron/repair wardrobe
— Shine shoes
— Get haircut, manicure
— Buy needed items and clothes
— Plan means of transportation and routes
— Find out if parking is available
— Estimate time needed for traveling to job
— Pick out first day's outfit
— Pack lunch
— Take glasses, pens, calculator
— Pack briefcase, pocketbook, wallet
— Set alarm

At the Job

— Repeat names to yourself/listen to names carefully
— Make notes of instructions as given
— Read protocols, rule books
— Obtain keys to office, washroom, desk
— Get equipment and supplies: calendar, phone list, stationery, adding machine, typewriter, lamp
— Fill out time card, medical insurance forms
— Find out where to eat lunch
— Ask about responsibilities, job definition, expectations
— Ask about chain of command
— Find out about benefits, regulations, rules
— Decorate office/set up desk/fix work area/set up tools
— Find fire exits

SEE ALSO:
WHAT TO HAVE IN AN OFFICE DESK (LIST 86)

32. Applying to College

Sometimes it seems as though you need a college degree to figure out how to apply to college. We hope this list will simplify matters.

__ Send in SAT and achievement test applications/ discuss costs of testing with parents

__ Sign up for SAT review course

__ Buy and study SAT review books

__ Discuss with parents finances available for college/ discuss costs of applying to many schools

__ Decide on size of school, educational philosophy, location, costs, types of students, types of courses

__ Buy/review books with descriptions of all colleges

__ Discuss career goals with parents, friends, counselors, teachers

__ Research scholarships, grants, financial aid

__ Discuss school choices with parents, friends, counselors, alumni

__ Go to college fairs/talk with representatives of desired schools

__ Send for college catalogues, applications

__ Check requirements of prospective schools: grades, minimum achievement scores, SAT scores, residency

__ Visit schools

__ Decide which schools you will apply to/discuss with parents

__ Make a chart of application requirements: filing deadlines, references, SAT scores, achievement tests, financial forms, transcripts

__ Decide on whom you will use as references/send forms

__ Fill out applications/financial aid applications

__ Make list of school achievements, clubs, extracurricular activities, interests

__ Write autobiography and personal essays/show to parents, friends, teachers

__ Type finished applications and essays

___ Make copies of all materials
___ Buy stamps/mail applications
___ Take SAT exams/have scores forwarded
___ Have high school transcripts forwarded
___ Arrange dates for interviews
___ Arrange transportation, lodging, meals
___ Prepare outfit for trip
___ Prepare questions about school/practice interviewing/discuss with friends your favorite books, career, goals
___ Pack
___ Visit dormitories, library, classrooms, student center, dining hall
___ Talk to students and faculty
___ Sit in on classes and student social activities
___ Speak further to colleges about financial aid
___ Find out about eligibility for college scholarships

SEE ALSO:
PACKING FOR COLLEGE/BOARDING SCHOOL (LIST 66)

33. Daily, Weekly, Monthly Chores

The way in which chores are done varies greatly from person to person, so you'll probably have to do a lot of tailoring of these lists.

The lists may be particularly helpful if you are leaving your home or apartment in someone else's care.

Daily

___ Make beds
___ Do dishes
___ Take out garbage
___ Take in milk, newspapers, mail
___ Feed animals
___ Take in garbage pails
___ Straighten up house, dust, sweep
___ Clean sink, tub
___ Check plants for watering
___ Check answering machine
___ Check calendar, lists
___ Buy needed food items
___ Water lawns and garden
___ Change water in vases
___ Plan menu/cook

Weekly

___ Shop for food
___ Clean house/wax floors
___ Clean stove
___ Clean animal boxes, cages
___ Do finances, banking
___ Wash clothes/check lint filters
___ Send in cleaning, laundry
___ Iron

___ Clean out refrigerator
___ Sweep front walk
___ Wash car
___ Weed yard, garden
___ Mow lawn
___ Check outdoor drains
___ Replenish fuel supplies/check boiler water
___ Check schedules for week: birthdays, appointments, dinner parties/buy needed gifts and cards
___ Plan entertainment schedule
___ Clean outdoor furniture
___ Polish shoes

Monthly

___ Defrost refrigerator
___ Wash windows
___ Feed house plants
___ Check smoke alarms
___ Clean out vacuum bags
___ Balance checkbook
___ Pay bills
___ Replace household/business supplies: stamps, cleaning equipment, lightbulbs
___ Scrub bathroom tiles
___ Clean appliances/check filters
___ Exterminate
___ Check clothes and shoes for repair
___ Polish silver
___ Sew/darn
___ Unclog drains
___ Wash off plant leaves
___ Check oil/water in car

SEE ALSO:
    SPRING CHORES (LIST 34) SUMMER CHORES (LIST 35)
    FALL CHORES (LIST 36) WINTER CHORES (LIST 37)
    CAR CARE (LIST 38) FOOD SHOPPING (LIST 87)

34. Spring Chores

__ Arrange semiannual medical and dental checkups
__ Remove snow tires
__ Remove weather stripping
__ Take off storm windows
__ Wash windows
__ Put up screens
__ Put in air conditioners/remove covers/clean filters/test
__ Unwrap pipes
__ Clean/oil/put away winter equipment: shovels, snow blower, sleds
__ Take out lawn mower and garden tools
__ Take out hoses
__ Turn on outdoor water
__ Remove leaves, winter debris
__ Uncover trees, shrubs
__ Fertilize soil, lawn
__ Turn over soil
__ Prepare seedlings
__ Plant
__ Weed garden, lawn
__ Trim bushes, trees
__ Take out/clean garden furniture
__ Take out grill/buy charcoal and fuel/buy paper plates, cups, napkins, table cloths, plastic utensils for barbeques
__ Take out sports gear: bicycles, badminton set, croquet set, golf clubs
__ Check/repair sports equipment: tennis rackets, rafts, life preservers, oars, boats, bicycles
__ Open outdoor outlets
__ Check for/exterminate termites, bugs
__ Check/repair winter damage to house/paint
__ Paint/repair outdoor furniture
__ Weatherproof outdoor wood surfaces, furniture
__ Check/repair roof
__ Check drains, gutters

- Plan summer vacation/send for brochures, maps, guidebooks
- Take out/try on/repair spring, summer clothes
- Put winter clothes in storage
- Clean closets/straighten drawers
- Spring cleaning: rugs, drapes, furniture, pantry, bedding, workshop, garden shed
- Wax floors
- Clean behind and under refrigerator/clean other appliances
- Repot house plants/feed regularly/put outdoors
- Check/clean fans, exhaust fans
- Clean/sand food-preparation surfaces
- Caulk tub, tiles
- Recement sidewalk cracks, loose bricks, tiles, stone wall
- Inspect pipes for leaks, corrosion/arrange for repairs
- Clean garage, basement, attic
- Plan garage sales, donations
- Check/lubricate motors in heating system
- Clean fuel tanks, wood stoves, furnace
- Clean/oil outdoor machinery: well and pool pumps
- Chop wood for winter/stack for drying
- Get car tuned
- Have yearly fire drill/do home safety check

SEE ALSO:
 DAILY, WEEKLY, MONTHLY CHORES (LIST 33)
 CAR CARE (LIST 38)

35. Summer Chores

__ Water yard, plants, lawn
__ Weed garden, mow lawn, prune plants
__ Clean air conditioner filters
__ Spray against insects
__ Feed plants
__ Clean lawn furniture
__ Remove cobwebs from outside of house
__ Harvest fruits, vegetables
__ Can and preserve fruits, vegetables
__ Dry herbs
__ Paint/repair house
__ Do unfinished spring tasks
__ Drain boiler water/overhaul heating system

SEE ALSO:
    DAILY, WEEKLY, MONTHLY CHORES (LIST 33)

36. Fall Chores

___ Arrange semiannual medical and dental checkups
___ Clean outside drains
___ Rake leaves
___ Clean out gutters
___ Take in indoor plants
___ Harvest fruits, vegetables
___ Can and preserve fruits, vegetables
___ Prune garden
___ Plant bulbs
___ Spray garden
___ Put mulch around plants
___ Cover bushes
___ Remove/clean screens
___ Cover air conditioner/remove
___ Wash windows
___ Put up storm windows
___ Put hoses away
___ Turn off outside water
___ Drain outdoor water pipes
___ Put away outdoor furniture
___ Clean/put away grill
___ Cover outdoor outlets
___ Overhaul lawn mower
___ Clean/oil/sharpen/put away gardening tools
___ Take out/try on/repair winter clothes
___ Clean closets/straighten drawers
___ Put summer clothes in storage
___ Take out quilts, blankets
___ Caulk windows
___ Weather-strip windows, doors
___ Insulate necessary areas: pipes, boiler
___ Clean/tune/check/lubricate heating system

___ Clean/check flues, chimneys
___ Clean/vacuum/check radiators, heaters, registers
___ Change filters in hot-air system
___ Set thermostat
___ Check/clean humidifiers
___ Restack/buy/check wood supply
___ Resume fuel deliveries
___ Winterize car
___ Weatherproof/polish boots

SEE ALSO:
DAILY, WEEKLY, MONTHLY CHORES (LIST 33)

37. Winter Chores

___ Check/take out space heaters
___ Repair/prepare skis, skates, sleds, ice-fishing gear, snowshoes, hockey gear
___ Tune up/repair snow blower, snowmobile
___ Take out shovel, ice chopper
___ Buy rock salt, sand
___ Put on snow tires, chains
___ Check antifreeze in car
___ Check boiler water, filters, fuel supply
___ Check pipes against frost
___ Set up new date book/enter birthdays, anniversaries
___ Oil/clean appliances, machinery, indoor pumps
___ Overhaul selected items: piano, sewing machine
___ Check/repair sports gear for spring: tennis racket, water skis
___ Sharpen axes, chain saw, knives
___ Mend screens
___ Check basement for dampness, mold
___ Update photograph album
___ Fix/sharpen/replace fishing tackle
___ Order seeds
___ Prepare/start spring seedlings
___ Prepare bills, checks, receipts for taxes

SEE ALSO:
  TAXES (LIST 15)
  DAILY/WEEKLY/MONTHLY CHORES (LIST 33)

38. Car Care

This list is written both for those who plan to do the maintenance work themselves and those (like us) who drive straight to a local mechanic.

General Preparations

___ Check owner's manuals for servicing schedules
___ Make list of what tasks you can do yourself
___ Buy automobile repair manual for your type of car
___ Buy needed replacement parts
___ Make appointment with mechanic
___ Enter record of car care in maintenance log
___ Have car inspected

Under the Hood

___ Tune up car
___ Change oil / replace oil filter
___ Drain radiator water / refill
___ Check antifreeze and coolant level / replace
___ Check brake fluid / replenish
___ Check transmission fluid / replenish
___ Refill windshield-washer reservoir
___ Examine rubber hoses / replace
___ Examine fan belt / tighten / replace
___ Check air conditioner
___ Test battery / replenish battery water
___ Sand battery cable connectors and terminals / coat with white grease
___ Check brakes and emergency brake
___ Check play in steering wheel / check power-steering fluid
___ Adjust clutch
___ Realign front end
___ Grease

Outside the Car

___ Check body for rust/repair
___ Wash/wax car/rustproof
___ Rotate tires/check for wear
___ Adjust tire pressure to load and season
___ Switch snow and regular tires
___ Check lugs for rust/loosen/retighten
___ Check snow chains
___ Replace windshield-wiper blades
___ Check all lights/replace bulbs

Inside the Car

___ Vacuum
___ Clean dashboard, steering wheel, rear-view mirror, windows and windshield
___ Empty ashtrays
___ Wash floor mats
___ Organize glove compartment
___ Check batteries in emergency flashlight
___ Replace fuses
___ Check emergency equipment: flares, air pump, fire extinguisher
___ Examine spare tire/check air pressure
___ Check jack, lug wrench
___ Put winter items in car: sand, scraper, shovel, salt, chains

39. Hiring Household Help

__ Make list of desired qualities: personality traits, cleaning abilities, cooking skills
__ Ask friends and family for referrals
__ Contact local and foreign agencies
__ Check with state employment bureaus
__ Put ads in newspapers
__ Check local newspapers and bulletin boards
__ Inquire locally: churches, merchants, schools
__ Make list of expected duties
__ Decide on salary, benefits, and vacations
__ Make appointment for interview
__ Give directions for transportation to your home
__ Check references/speak to previous employers
__ Check work permits and alien registration cards
__ Check to see if person is bonded
__ Check qualifications for special needs (for example, licensed practical nurse)
__ Discuss specific tasks and responsibilities
__ Specify objects not to be touched or cleaned
__ Discuss expectations: hours, punctuality, use of television, food provided
__ Discuss salary, raises, vacations
__ Decide about uniforms
__ Discuss child-rearing practices
__ Determine hours, days off
__ Ask about special needs: medical restrictions, diets, allergies
__ Set up probationary period
__ Show accommodations/buy needed items: beds, dressers, linens, toiletries
__ Explain how to operate appliances, equipment
__ Show where tools are kept
__ Observe person work
__ Observe person's behavior with children and pets
__ Hire/make written contract
__ Arrange social security payments, workmen's compensation, insurance

40. Before You Go

When we were children, whenever the family left the house for a trip, grandmother would say as we got a block or two from home, "Did I turn off the gas on the stove?" We'd always turn around and go back to check. The gas was always off. This list is dedicated to her, although no doubt if we'd had the list then, she would have asked, "Did I check the whole list?"

Home

___ Arrange to have plants watered/write list of instructions
___ Arrange for pet care/make list of instructions
___ Contact animal shelter or kennel/make reservations
___ Arrange for lawn, garden to be tended
___ Arrange to have garbage pails brought back to house
___ Arrange to have heating system tended
___ Arrange to have sidewalk shoveled
___ Stop newspaper delivery/ask neighbor to take in papers
___ Stop milk, soda deliveries
___ Rearrange long-term deliveries scheduled during your trip
___ Have mail forwarded or held at post office
___ Notify police, security personnel, superintendent that you will be away
___ Leave alarm instructions and alarm key with neighbor, police, superintendent
___ Leave extra house keys and emergency numbers with neighbors, family, superintendent
___ Put valuables in safekeeping
___ Set up automatic light timers
___ Put new bulbs in lights to be left on

___ Disconnect telephone/hook up answering machine
___ Empty perishables from refrigerator/defrost
___ Leave refrigerator door open if refrigerator is turned off
___ Turn down refrigerator thermostat if refrigerator is kept on
___ Turn down heating thermostat
___ Disconnect appliances from wall sockets: radio, television, toaster, stereo, washing machine
___ Turn off faucets to washing machine, outdoor hoses
___ Check pilot lights
___ Secure windows and window locks
___ Straighten house/wash dishes
___ Take out garbage
___ Check that all doors are locked: cellar, basement, garage, front, side back, porch, attic to roof

Subletting

___ Remove valuables, keepsakes
___ Ask neighbor or friend to be advisor in case of emergency
___ Leave extra set of keys with neighbor or friend
___ Leave list of emergency numbers: plumber, electrician, neighbor, where you can be reached
___ Clean out some closets and drawers for subletter's use
___ Show space to subletter/explain use of appliances/ show location of cleaning equipment
___ State your expectations: condition of house for return, food and supplies to be waiting
___ Write out instructions for operating appliances, watering plants, pet care, garden needs, mail, garbage pickup
___ Make list of chores needed to be done daily, weekly, monthly
___ Strip beds/leave linens
___ Make extra set of keys/give tenant keys

Personal Arrangements

___ Make appointments with doctors, dentists
___ Renew prescriptions/get travel medication

- Have eyeglasses fixed/get new pair
- Check condition of luggage/buy luggage
- Select clothing to be taken
- Buy needed items: clothes, accessories, drug and personal items
- Wash/repair/iron clothes
- Shine/repair shoes
- Take in cleaning/pick up
- Prepare outfits needed for day after return: clothes for first day of work
- Check equipment: skis, tennis racket, camera/replace
- Get haircut, manicure
- Return library books
- Pay bills
- Arrange to have bills paid while you are away
- Make good-bye calls
- Pack
- Check that you have keys, directions, tickets, itinerary

SEE ALSO:
TRAVEL ARRANGEMENTS (LIST 41)

WHAT-TO-DO CHECK √ LISTS
Vacations

41. Travel Arrangements

__ Consult travel agent
__ Ask friends for advice
__ Plan itinerary
__ Get pictures for passport
__ File passport application and visa applications
__ Get vaccinations
__ Get international driver's license
__ Check with hotels about meal plans, special rates, services, physical layout
__ Make reservations for hotels, motels, campgrounds
__ Reserve rental car
__ Reserve travel tickets for airplanes, boats, trains
__ Notify airlines, trains, boats, hotels, of special needs: diet, children, handicap, medical problems
__ Buy tickets/send deposits/pick up tickets
__ Leave itinerary and hotel addresses with person forwarding your mail
__ Visit tourist bureaus/get special passes and schedules for museums, tours, sites, concerts
__ Research information and regulations of area to be visited
__ Arrange special events: sailing, scuba diving, hikes
__ Buy books: language books, guides, dictionaries
__ Buy maps
__ Buy travel insurance/update will
__ Arrange child care
__ Put car in garage/leave with friend or family
__ Buy traveler's checks/exchange currency/get money for tips, cab fare from airport or dock
__ Give friend or relative traveler's-check numbers
__ Confirm reservations for travel, hotel, car rental
__ Arrange transportation to boat, plane, train
__ Pack suitcases and carry-on bags
__ Pack food

SEE ALSO: BEFORE YOU GO (LIST 40) WHEN YOU RETURN (LIST 42) PREPARING/PACKING CAR FOR TRIP (LIST 60)

42. When You Return

— Unlock/open windows/air out house
— Check heating system/turn on air conditioner
— Unpack/arrange drawers and closets
— Put away luggage, sports gear, luggage carrier
— Water plants
— Reset thermostat
— Call family, friends
— Notify police, security personnel, superintendant, neighbors of your return
— Make beds/put out clean towels
— Disconnect automatic light timer
— Reconnect appliances to wall sockets
— Play back messages from answering machine/ reconnect telephone
— Check mail
— Turn on faucets to washing machine, outdoor hose
— Do laundry
— Get car from garage or friend
— Take clothes to cleaners
— Take film for developing
— Cash in traveler's checks/exchange foreign currency
— Go to personal bank/make deposits, withdrawals
— Get back valuables from safety-deposit box or storage
— Get mail from post office
— Shop for food and household supplies
— Get pet from kennel, friend, family member
— Reset refrigerator temperature control
— Put away food
— Dust
— Sweep/shovel sidewalk
— Mow lawn/weed garden
— Wash car/clean interior

__ Get back extra keys from neighbor, superintendent, family member

__ Get back alarm key

__ Start soda, milk, food deliveries

__ Start newspaper delivery

__ Call household help/set up schedule

__ Make appointments for haircuts, manicures

__ Inspect house

__ Review appointment book

__ Prepare outfit for next day's work, school, appointments

__ Get work material in order

__ Pay bills

__ Write thank-you notes to caretakers, hosts, business associates

__ Put together notes from trip/edit diary

__ Catch up on mail, newspapers, magazines

__ Get keys from subletter

__ Return subletter's deposit

43. Renting A Vacation Home

An allergic friend of ours once rented a beautiful vacation home in Vermont. Unfortunately, he forgot to ask if the owners had pets. Although the owners took their three collies away with them, our friend spent his first two weeks in misery while he vacuumed away all the dog hairs. These two lists consist of questions: the first, those to ask before you rent the house; the second, before you pack for the vacation.

___ Decide on distance from home
___ Make decision on desired features: lake, woods, beach
___ Register with agents
___ Read newspaper ads
___ Check with family and friends
___ Ask people who have been to area if they know of houses available
___ Decide if you want to share house
___ Decide how much you can afford
___ Ask for pictures of house
___ Visit area/check house

Ask Owner or Real Estate Agent about the Following:

___ Size of house, size of rooms
___ Location
___ Price/when to pay money/is sharing acceptable
___ Lease
___ Security and provisions for its return
___ Who pays utilities
___ Is telephone installed
___ Sleeping facilities, firmness of mattresses
___ Appliances: dishwasher, washing machine, dryer, television, iron, refrigerator

___ Heating system, fireplaces, air conditioners
___ Proximity to lakes, beaches, pool, hiking trails
___ Neighbors
___ Proximity to road, heavy traffic
___ Shady, sunny areas around house
___ Decks, views
___ Boats, docking facilities
___ Sports facilities: tennis courts, volleyball net, horseback riding
___ Local facilities, activities, religious institutions, shopping, theaters, movies
___ Proximity to problem or noisy areas: dump, children's camp, teenage hangout, drive-in movies
___ Mosquitos, flies, other pest problems
___ Pets, poison ivy, allergy problems
___ Availability of laundromat, dry cleaning
___ Availability of babysitters
___ Availability of newspapers, books, magazines
___ Local ordinances: pets on beach, open fires
___ Beach stickers, dumping permits, car parking
___ Access in snow
___ Water levels, algae, pollution, motor boats
___ All items on Outfitting a Rented Vacation House (list 53)
___ Quirks in plumbing, appliances
___ Whom to contact in case of emergency: plumber, electrician, nearest neighbor, police
___ How to order extra fuel, gas
___ Instructions on gardening, plant care
___ Starting and leaving dates
___ Directions to house
___ Where to get key

44. Opening Summer House

We've tried to order this list with essential chores first, less critical ones last. But our sense of what's important is probably different from yours, so delete and add to create your own list.

—— Have phone turned on
—— Have electricity turned on
—— Have water turned on
—— Have gas turned on
—— Check/order bottled gas
—— Check appliances/turn on
—— Ignite pilot lights
—— Remove protective pipe coverings
—— Check fuel supply/refill
—— Have chimney checked
—— Check boiler water/turn on boiler
—— Check well and water pump
—— Reset thermostat
—— Set clocks
—— Check fire extinguishers, smoke alarms
—— Remove storm windows, protective coverings
—— Put up screens
—— Check air conditioners/clean filters
—— Open windows/air out house
—— Air out bedding, mattresses
—— Empty rodent traps
—— Dust/vacuum/clean/wash house
—— Remove cobwebs
—— Wash drapes and spreads
—— Unpack
—— Make beds
—— Make shopping list
—— Shop for food, household supplies

___ Notify stores, post office, neighbors, police of your arrival
___ Arrange for deliveries: food, newspaper
___ Arrange garbage pickup/get town dump sticker
___ Get town passes, beach stickers
___ Uncover outdoor sockets/put in lightbulbs
___ Set up equipment for children, pets
___ Take out hoses
___ Take out grill
___ Put out lawn furniture
___ Set up clotheslines
___ Put out/check awnings
___ Set up hammock, swing
___ Uncover/clean/fill pool
___ Put out dock
___ Inflate sports gear, rafts
___ Set out boat
___ Review safety rules with children
___ Clean out gutters, drains
___ Check house for leaks, repairs/arrange for necessary
___ Uncover shrubs
___ Check/repair/oil/take out equipment: lawn mower, sports gear
___ Rake leaves/work in garden/call gardener
___ Start garden
___ Paint/repair

SEE ALSO: SPRING CHORES (LIST 34) SUMMER CHORES (LIST 35) BEFORE YOU GO (LIST 40) PUTTING A BOAT IN THE WATER (LIST 48) PUTTING A BOAT TO BED (LIST 49)

45. Closing a Summer House

Those items that can be done ahead of time are at the beginning of the list; last minute items are at the end. Our sense of priorities may differ from yours, so read through and make your own order.

___ Deflate/put away sports gear, rafts, swings, children's equipment
___ Put away lawn mower, grill, hammock, other yard items
___ Put away boat
___ Pull dock out of water/put away
___ Empty/clean/cover pool
___ Put away lawn furniture
___ Cover shrubs/mulch around plants
___ Repair screens
___ Remove awnings
___ Put away hoses
___ Take down clothesline
___ Put protective coverings on pipes
___ Check/clean gutters, drains
___ Check house for needed repairs/arrange to have work done
___ Weatherproof
___ Remove outdoor lightbulbs/cover outdoor sockets
___ Cover/remove air conditioners
___ Remove/clean drapes, spreads, rugs
___ Get cartons for packing
___ Stop deliveries
___ Stop garbage pickups
___ Return library books
___ Return borrowed items
___ Pick up clothes from laundry, dry cleaner
___ Have mail forwarded
___ Have phone disconnected
___ Arrange winter watch of home

__ Leave key with neighbor, police, caretaker
__ Let police, neighbors, stores know of your departure
__ Arrange for plant care/pack plants
__ Put away/camphorize blankets, linens, bedding
__ Defrost refrigerator
__ Remove all food items, perishables, rodent temptations
__ Hide valuables, stereo, television
__ Dismantle items that go with you
__ Check drawers, closets, hamper
__ Pack
__ Close chimney damper/clean out fireplace
__ Straighten/clean house
__ Clean garbage/make final trip to dump
__ Set rodent traps
__ Shut down boiler
__ Reset thermostat
__ Remove screens
__ Put up storm windows and doors, protective window coverings
__ Lock windows
__ Disconnect appliances, clocks/leave refrigerator door open
__ Turn off gas
__ Turn water off/drain pipes
__ Turn off electricity/turn out lights
__ Set alarm system
__ Lock house, garage, sheds

SEE ALSO:
   FALL CHORES (LIST 36)
   WINTER CHORES (LIST 37)
   WHEN YOU RETURN (LIST 42)

46. Being a House Guest

There are many differences in entertaining style, ranging from formal to informal, private to public. Respect the style of the people you're staying with and let the list follow.

___ Arrange/confirm arrival time
___ Let hosts know of important data: allergies, medical problems, diets, handicaps
___ Check about pets, children
___ Ask if you should bring bedding, pillows, towels, beach towels, soap, shampoo, toothpaste
___ Buy/bring gift
___ Take along necessary medications, special foods
___ Ask about peculiarities of house: hot-water limitations, quirky appliances, plumbing needs
___ Ask about wakeup time, meal times, daily schedules
___ Offer to take hosts for dinner/offer to pay for shopping
___ Offer to help with chores
___ Straighten room/make bed
___ Offer to give host some time alone
___ Check about night lights, alarm clock
___ Ask about stripping bedding when you leave
___ Send thank-you note afterwards

47. Having a House Guest

Some people like house guests to accommodate themselves to their hosts' style; others prefer the refreshing change of new ways of doing things while their guests are with them. Whatever your choice, remember that hosting is an art built upon attention to detail, and many of those details are listed here.

— Arrange arrival time
— Let guests know if blankets, pillows, bedding, towels, beach towels are needed
— Ask about special food needs: allergies, diets, medical problems, handicaps
— Send travel directions
— Check household supplies, equipment
— Clean out closet, drawer space
— Plan meals/shop
— Plan entertainment, activities, introductions
— Get tickets, reservations for dinner, concerts, shows
— Estimate expenses/discuss sharing costs
— Prepare sleeping quarters
— Put out clean towels
— Show guests house
— Show guests their room, closets, drawer space
— Offer clock, books, tissues, night light
— Let guests know peculiarities of house: plumbing, hot-water limitations, appliance quirks
— Discuss expectations about meal times, routines, chores, time alone
— Discuss wake-up routine and breakfast
— Let guests know the level of formality you expect
— Provide guests with maps of area
— Discuss transportation, use of car
— Provide house keys/arrange meeting time if spending time apart
— Explain local, national customs
— Tell guests what to do with bedding when leaving
— Arrange transportation for departure

48. Putting a Boat in the Water

Boats, like homes, require upkeep even if they are supposedly "maintenance free." We hope these lists on boat care will enable you to spend more time enjoying your boat and less time working on it.

Preparations

— Make a list of necessary work/set priorities
— Check weather reports for scheduling indoor or outdoor work
— Schedule work that boat yard needs to do
— Schedule day for putting boat in water
— Order cleaning and boating supplies/buy tools, sandpaper, brushes, paints, varnish, lubricating oil

Cabin Work

— Throw out accumulated junk
— Wash woodwork
— Clean stove, sink, cabinets
— Check stove for grease buildup/check fittings
— Deodorize ice chest/clean
— Clean/rehang curtains
— Air bedding, cushions
— Inspect flooring, mats
— Check/replace dishes, utensils, cooking equipment
— Make list of provisions needed
— Examine screens/repair
— Examine locks/apply graphite
— Adjust clocks/check barometer/check compass

Interior Work

___ Scour/repaint bilge
___ Wash bulkheads
___ Check bilge pump/repair
___ Close out bilge openings, drain holes
___ Wash/repaint engine area
___ Drain antifreeze in head
___ Repair leaks in head
___ Check plumbing
___ Check hoses/check/grease seacocks
___ Check/replace hose clamps
___ Plane door, lockers, hatch covers
___ Refinish woodwork
___ Polish metalwork

Hull Work

___ Clean sides/wax
___ Examine/repair gel coat
___ Check for dry rot, other problems
___ Caulk/pay seams
___ Check for loose planks
___ Repaint
___ Wash portholes with fresh water/examine for leaks
___ Paint bottom

Deck Work

___ Clean/replace/repaint canvas
___ Examine fastenings and fittings: cleats, bitts
___ Refinish bright work: handrails, cabin sides
___ Polish metalwork: bell, foghorn
___ Examine/repair skylights
___ Examine/repair ladders
___ Check/tighten flagpoles and fittings

Electrical Work

___ Inspect wiring/check fuses/test lights
___ Clean/test horn

- Clean/test searchlight
- Inspect/repair radio
- Check/repair pumps
- Examine/test fans
- Examine/clean switches, contact points

Engine Work

- Recharge/install battery
- Clean/grease battery terminal poles
- Top up battery water
- Clean out tanks/fill with clean fuel
- Check fuel lines for leaks/clean fuel filters
- Replace oil/change oil filter
- Clean/grease engine
- Tune up engine/schedule tune-up by boat yard
- Examine/repair gears, exhaust system, hoses
- Check propeller, stuffing box, strut bearings
- Tighten nuts, bolts, screws
- Check gauges
- Check hose connections

Miscellaneous

- Wash/repaint dinghy
- Check all surfaces for corrosion/varnish/paint
- Recharge fire extingusihers
- Inspect life jackets, raft
- Examine/replace distress signal kit: flares, flags, mirror, dye marker
- Check/repair anchor, chains, line
- Examine/repair sails
- Clean flags
- Clean boat of fire hazards: paint, oily rags, paper, turpentine
- Make list/buy supplies
- Make inventory list/make storage plan for all gear
- Inspect/lubricate wheel, tiller lines, sheaves, quadrants
- Overhaul davits
- Check/repair winter cover

49. Putting a Boat to Bed

Preparations

___ Ask experienced boat owners their opinion of the boat yard you plan to use
___ Check insurance coverage of boat yard: fire, theft, liability, damage
___ Determine what boat yard will and won't do
___ Make list of repairs for boat yard to do/make list of ones you'll do
___ Find out what boat yard wants you to do with fuel tanks
___ Order repairs/get written contract
___ Schedule day to have boat hauled
___ Ask someone to inspect work periodically if you can't
___ Visit regularly
___ Review spring chores/do if weather permits

Cabin Work

___ Remove perishables: books, dishes, food, clothing, sails, outboard motor, cooking, fuel, lightbulbs
___ Remove valuable items
___ Survey galley gear/make list of items to be replaced
___ Remove all broken, worn, or useless material
___ Clean galley gear/replace
___ Clean ice box/put in deodorizer
___ Clean lockers
___ Oil hinges
___ Winterize sink plumbing
___ Clean/winterize head
___ Launder/repair curtains, drapes, bedding, linen
___ Air/clean cushions
___ Clean upholstery
___ Wash cabin floor covering
___ Check/resand doors, drawers
___ check/repaint cabin woodwork
___ Repair/refinish cabin hardware

Engine Work

___ Schedule repair work with yard/order parts
___ Drain/replace engine oil
___ Put antifreeze in engine
___ Drain fuel lines, fuel tank
___ Remove batteries/store in warm place/refill battery
water/recharge
___ Clean/grease battery cable terminals
___ Clean/repaint engine
___ Wash/lubricate moving parts with fresh water
___ Put petroleum jelly on all exposed corrodable parts
___ Overhaul dinghy outboard motor

Hull Work

___ Cradle/block/shore boat
___ Scrub bottom
___ Refinish/paint bottom
___ Give hull protective coating
___ Check/repair rudder
___ Check/repair propeller

Deck Work

___ Clean deck
___ Paint/varnish
___ Replace/repaint canvas deck covering
___ Check wheel/examine shaft bearings/send for refitting
___ Check deck hardware for weakness/send for refitting

Miscellaneous

___ Examine/clean/store/repair sails
___ Check/repair sail covers, other canvas
___ Repair/launder flags, pennants
___ Check ground tackle, mooring pennant, mooring buoy
___ Remove/revarnish/cover mast
___ Inspect/clean water tanks

__ Clean/drain/paint bilge
__ Repair/repaint dinghy
__ Varnish oars
__ Varnish spreaders
__ Varnish poles
__ Clean/repair/adjust navigational equipment
__ Repair/adjust/polish navigation lights
__ Clean/repair electric accessories/test electric system
__ Inspect/repair pumps
__ Repair/refinish sea anchor
__ Get tools ready for spring work
__ Clean paintbrushes
__ Make list of needed supplies, parts, stores/order
__ Make list of all items to be returned to boat
__ Check winter cover, lashings
__ Open doors, hatches, ports, lids, drawers for ventilation
__ Cover boat

50. Packing a Carry-on Bag

Accessories and Personal Gear

___ Money/wallet/foreign currency/credit cards/ checkbook
___ Traveler's checks
___ Passport/visas/international driver's license
___ Identification/medical alert cards
___ Tickets/reservation receipts/itinerary/maps
___ Books/magazines/guidebooks
___ Work from office/correspondence
___ Date book/address book
___ Pens/paper/stationery
___ Calculator
___ Tape recorder/tape
___ Watch
___ Keys
___ Cigarettes/pipe gear/lighter
___ Eyeglasses/sunglasses/contact lenses/lens cleanser
___ Camera/film/flash
___ Umbrella/rain gear
___ Pocket knife

Clothes and Toiletries

___ Shawl/sweater/jacket
___ Extra outfit in case luggage gets lost
___ Brush/comb
___ Toothbrush/toothpaste
___ Shaving gear/soap
___ Cosmetics/compact/perfume
___ Emery board
___ Tissues

Miscellaneous

___ Food
___ Breakables
___ Gifts
___ Deck of cards/games
___ Gum/candy
___ Toothpicks/dental floss
___ Lip balm/breath freshener
___ Medications

51. Packing for a Trip Abroad

If you are traveling with someone else, we suggest you share the suitcases. If one gets waylaid, you'll both have clothing in the other. Also, consider weight when you pack—both in relation to airline regulations and how much you can carry if you can't find a porter. Inquire as to whether items you may need are available in the country you're traveling to, things like film for your camera or medications for yourself.

Don't forget to leave room in your luggage for the gifts you will inevitably buy for family and friends.

Men's Clothing

___ Underpants
___ T-shirts
___ Socks: sport/dress
___ Shirts
___ Pants: dress/casual
___ Sport jacket
___ Suit
___ Evening clothes: tuxedo
___ Ties/ascot
___ Polos/turtlenecks
___ Dungarees
___ Shorts
___ Sweaters/vests
___ Belt/suspenders/garters
___ Tie pin/jewelry/cuff links
___ Handkerchiefs
___ Pajamas
___ Robe
___ Sportswear: jogging suit/supporter/sweat band/tennis outfit/sweat shirt/goggles

___ Bathing suit
___ Bathing suit top/robe
___ Bathing cap
___ Jacket/outerwear
___ Overcoat
___ Raincoat
___ Hat/cap
___ Scarf/muffler
___ Gloves
___ Shoes: dress/casual/sandals/walking
___ Boots/rubbers
___ Sneakers
___ Slippers
___ Shower/beach shoes
___ Extra shoelaces

Women's Clothing

___ Underpants
___ Brassieres/undershirts
___ Garter belt/garters
___ Girdle
___ Stockings/panty hose/peds
___ Socks: sport/dress
___ Slips
___ Blouses/tops
___ Skirts
___ Pants: dress/casual
___ Dresses
___ Suits
___ Evening clothes: gowns
___ Polos/turtlenecks
___ Dungarees
___ Shorts
___ Halters
___ Sweaters/vest
___ Accessories: scarves
___ Belts/sashes
___ Jewelry
___ Handkerchiefs

- __ Nightgowns/pajamas
- __ Robe
- __ Sportswear: jogging suit/sweat band/tennis outfit/ sweat shirt/goggles/running bra
- __ Bathing suit
- __ Bathing suit top/robe
- __ Bathing cap
- __ Jacket/outerwear
- __ Overcoat/stole
- __ Raincoat
- __ Hats
- __ Scarves/wraps
- __ Gloves
- __ Pocketbook
- __ Evening purse
- __ Shoes: dress/casual/sandals/walking
- __ Boots/rubbers
- __ Sneakers
- __ Slippers
- __ Shower/beach shoes

Personal Effects and Toiletries

- __ Toothbrush/toothpaste
- __ Comb/brush
- __ Barrettes/ribbons/rollers/clips/rubber bands/bobby pins/hair spray
- __ Hair dryer
- __ Shower cap
- __ Wigs/wig box
- __ Shaving gear: razor/blades/shaving cream/brush/ after-shave lotion/electric razor/cord/styptic pencil
- __ Soap
- __ Shampoo
- __ Deodorant
- __ Skin lotions/creams/other toiletries/cleansers
- __ Perfumes/colognes
- __ Cosmetics: powder/rouge/lipstick/eye makeup/ eyelashes/lash curler
- __ Mirror

___ Manicure/nail equipment
___ Tweezer/scissors
___ Bleaches/depilatories/hair coloring
___ Lip balm
___ Tissues/cotton balls/toilet tissues
___ Cotton swabs
___ Sanitary pads/belt/tampons
___ Contraceptives
___ Medical appliances: braces/trusses/elastic bandages
___ Dentures/case/cleaner
___ First-aid kit/thermometer
___ Aspirin/Dramamine
___ Prescribed or other medications: antibiotics, antidiarrheal
___ Toothpicks/dental floss
___ Insect repellent
___ Suntan lotion

Accessories

___ Suitcase/knapsack/day pack
___ Wallet/money clip/pocketbook/passport case/money belt
___ Passports/visas
___ Money/traveler's checks/credit cards/checkbook/bank letter/foreign currency
___ Currency converter
___ Travel tickets
___ IDs/licenses/international driver's license/translated medical alert cards/medical insurance cards
___ Vaccination/innoculation certificates
___ Date book/address book
___ Address/phone numbers of embassies, consulates
___ Diary/ledger book
___ Pens/paper
___ Briefcase/attaché case
___ Work from office/home/correspondence
___ Directions/reservations/hotel receipts/car reservation/travel itineraries
___ Guidebooks/foreign-language books
___ Maps/information about area

- __ Watch
- __ House keys
- __ Eyeglasses/extra pair/eyeglass strap/eyeglass case/ lens cleaner
- __ Contact lenses/cleaning equipment
- __ Sunglasses
- __ Umbrella
- __ Calculator
- __ Electricity converter
- __ Traveling clock/alarm
- __ Travel iron
- __ Camera/film/flash
- __ Flashlight/extra batteries
- __ Sewing kit
- __ Shoe-shine equipment/shoetrees
- __ Hangers
- __ Laundry bag
- __ Detergent
- __ Plastic bags (for wet clothes)
- __ Towel/washcloth
- __ Travel clothesline/clothespins
- __ Sports gear: tennis racket/balls/skis/Frisbee/fishing gear
- __ Hobbies: knitting/musical instruments
- __ Books/cards/games/magazines
- __ Personal items: pictures/teddy bear/good-luck charm
- __ Radio/batteries
- __ Tape recorder/tapes/batteries/earphones
- __ Pocket knife
- __ Compass
- __ Luggage carrier/straps
- __ Liquor
- __ Cigarettes/pipe/lighter
- __ Equipment for pets
- __ List for repacking

SEE ALSO: BEFORE YOU GO (LIST 40) TRAVEL ARRANGE-
MENTS (LIST 41) WHEN YOU RETURN (LIST 42)

52. Packing for a Vacation in a Cold Climate

Men's Clothing

___ Underpants
___ T-shirts
___ Long underwear
___ Socks: sport/dress/thermal
___ Cross-country socks/gaiters
___ Shirts
___ Pants: dress/casual
___ Cross-country knickers
___ Sport jacket
___ Suit
___ Evening clothes: tuxedo
___ Ties/ascot
___ Polos/turtlenecks
___ Dungarees
___ Sweaters/vests
___ Belt/suspenders/garters
___ Tie pin/jewelry/cuff links
___ Handkerchiefs
___ Pajamas
___ Robe
___ Sportswear: jogging suit/athletic supporter/sweat
    band/tennis outfit/sweat shirt/goggles/skating outfit
___ Bathing suit
___ Bathing suit top/robe
___ Bathing cap
___ Jacket/outerwear/ski jacket/windbreaker
___ Ski pants/warm pants
___ Overcoat
___ Raincoat
___ Hat/cap/earmuffs
___ Scarf/muffler

— Ski mask
— Gloves/mittens
— Shoes: dress/casual
— Warm boots/rubbers/after-ski boots/hiking boots/
   weatherproof boots/cross-country shoes
— Sneakers
— Slippers
— Shower/pool shoes

Women's Clothing

— Underpants
— Brassieres/undershirts
— Garter belt/garters
— Long underwear
— Girdle
— Stockings/panty hose/peds
— Socks: sport/dress/thermal
— Cross-country socks/gaiters
— Slips
— Blouses/tops
— Skirts
— Pants: dress/casual
— Cross-country knickers
— Dresses
— Suits
— Evening clothes: gowns
— Polos/turtlenecks
— Dungarees
— Sweaters/vests
— Accessories: scarves
— Belts/sashes/suspenders
— Jewelry
— Handkerchiefs
— Nightgowns/pajamas
— Robe
— Sportswear: jogging suit/sweat band/tennis outfit/
   sweat shirt/goggles/skating outfit/running bra
— Bathing suit

___ Bathing suit top/robe
___ Bathing cap
___ Jacket/outerwear/ski jacket/windbreaker
___ Ski pants/warm pants
___ Overcoat/stole
___ Raincoat
___ Hats/earmuffs
___ Scarves/wraps
___ Ski mask
___ Gloves/mittens
___ Pocketbook
___ Evening purse
___ Shoes: dress/casual
___ Warm boots/rubbers/after-ski boots/hiking boots/
weatherproof boots/cross-country shoes
___ Sneakers
___ Slippers
___ Shower/pool shoes

Personal Effects/and Toiletries

___ Toothbrush/toothpaste
___ Comb/brush
___ Barrettes/ribbons/rollers/clips/rubber bands/bobby
pins
___ Hair dryer
___ Shower cap
___ Wigs/wig box
___ Shaving gear: razor/blades/shaving cream/brush/
after-shave lotion/electric razor/cord/styptic pencil
___ Soap
___ Shampoo
___ Deodorant
___ Skin lotions/creams/other toiletries/cleansers
___ Suntan lotion
___ Perfumes/colognes
___ Mirror
___ Cosmetics: powder/rouge/lipstick/eye makeup/
eyelashes/lash curler
___ Manicure/nail equipment

- Tweezer/scissors
- Bleaches/depilatories/hair coloring
- Lip balm
- Tissues/cotton balls/toilet tissues
- Cotton swabs
- Sanitary pads/belt/tampons
- Contraceptives
- Medical appliances: braces/elastic bandages/trusses
- Dentures/container/cleaner
- First-aid kit/thermometer
- Aspirin/Dramamine
- Prescribed or other medications
- Toothpicks/dental floss
- Spot-remover kit
- Extra shoelaces

Accessories

- Suitcase/knapsack
- Wallet/money clip/pocketbook
- Money/traveler's checks/credit cards/checkbook
- Travel tickets
- ID's/licenses/medical insurance cards/medical alert cards
- Date book/address book
- Diary/ledger book
- Pens/paper
- Briefcase/attaché case
- Work from office/home/correspondence
- Day pack
- Directions/reservations/receipts/ski tow tickets/rental car receipts
- Watch
- House keys
- Eyeglasses/extra pair/eyeglasses strap/ski goggles/lens cleaner
- Contact lenses/cleaning equipment
- Sunglasses
- Umbrella
- Calculator

__ Lighter/matches in waterproof container/cigarettes/
pipe gear
__ Traveling clock/alarm
__ Travel iron
__ Camera/film/film mailers/flash
__ Flashlight/batteries
__ Sewing kit/spot removal kit
__ Shoe-shine equipment/shoetrees/extra shoelaces
__ Hangers
__ Laundry bag
__ Plastic bags (for wet clothes)
__ Towels/washcloth
__ Sports gear: tennis racket/balls/toboggan/cross-
country skis/skis/ski boots/poles/sled/snowshoes/
skates/ski wax/bindings
__ Hobbies: knitting/musical instruments
__ Books/cards/games/magazines
__ Personal items: pictures/teddy bear/good-luck charm
__ Maps/information about area/compass
__ Radio/batteries
__ Tape recorder/tapes/earphones
__ Liquor
__ Ski rack
__ Luggage carrier
__ List for repacking

If Abroad

__ Passport/passport holder
__ Visas
__ Guidebooks/foreign-language books
__ Currency converter
__ Innoculations/vaccination certificate
__ Currency for arrival in country of destination
__ Electricity converter
__ Medication: antidiarrheal, antibiotic

SEE ALSO: BEFORE YOU GO (LIST 40) TRAVEL
ARRANGEMENTS (LIST 41) WHEN YOU RETURN (LIST 42)
PREPARING/PACKING CAR FOR TRIP (LIST 60)

53. Outfitting a Rented Vacation Home

If you like to cook, it can be disastrous to arrive at a rented vacation home and find that there are no sharp knives. We suggest using this list as a reference guide when you contact the landlord to ask what is provided.

Preparations

— Check with landlord about garbage pickup, fuel supply, emergency repair telephone numbers
— Ask landlord for appliance operating instructions
— Inquire about beach stickers, town rules, information about area
— Get keys and directions

Kitchen

— Dishes
— Serving dishes/bowls/salad bowl
— Mugs/cups/glasses
— Silverware
— Utensils: garlic press/measuring spoons/meat thermometer/corkscrew/can opener/vegetable peeler/nutcracker/grater/pastry brush/slotted spoon/potato masher/bottle opener/spatula/measuring cups
— Sharp knives/sharpening stone
— Salad spinner
— Pots/pans
— Wok
— Baking equipment: bread pans/pie pans/cake pans/sifter/rolling pin/mixing bowls/pastry cloth/cookie cutters/cookie press

__ Colander/strainer
__ Coffeepot/teapot
__ Pot holders/aprons
__ Appliances: blender/food processor/coffee grinder/
electric frying pan/toaster/electric mixer/juicer
__ Timer
__ Sugar bowl/butter dish/creamer
__ Juice container/pitcher/juice squeezer
__ Bread basket/trays/cutting board
__ Ice bucket/tongs
__ Cooler/thermos
__ Spices/staples
__ Pepper mill
__ Food containers
__ Sponges/cleaning equipment
__ Broom/dust pan
__ Cook books/recipes

Linens

__ Sheets/pillowcases/mattress covers
__ Towels/washcloths
__ Beach towels
__ Dishtowels
__ Tablecloths/napkins/place mats
__ Blankets/beach blankets
__ Bedspreads
__ Bath mat
__ Pillows
__ Shower curtain

Outdoor Gear

__ Barbeque grill/grill utensils/fire starter
__ Lawn chairs/beach chairs
__ Hammock
__ Clothesline/clothespins
__ Children's equipment: toddler pool/swing/play pen
__ Sports gear: bicycles/boats/softballs, bats, mitts/
badminton set/croquet set/Frisbee/volleyball and net

Miscellaneous

___ Television/radio/stereo system/tape deck
___ Records/tapes
___ Alarm clock
___ Hangers
___ Iron
___ Special items: food scale if dieting/board for under mattress/bathroom scale/Waterpik
___ Decorating items: art works/vases/candlesticks/candles/rugs/curtains
___ Plants
___ Pet equipment: cage/litter box and litter/leash/collar/chain
___ Pens/papers/typewriter/scissors/tape/glue/pencil sharpener/stationery/stamps
___ Games/cards/books
___ Tool kit/ax/hatchet
___ Picnic basket/tote bags/day packs
___ Fire extinguisher/first-aid kit
___ Lists for repacking

SEE ALSO:
  WHAT TO HAVE IN A KITCHEN (LIST 77)
  FOOD SHOPPING (LIST 87)

PACKING CHECK√LISTS
Vacations

54. Packing for a Summer Vacation in the Country

You can use this list in conjunction with Outfitting a Rented Vacation Home (list 53) if you need to bring along household items to your vacation spot.

Leisure Gear

___ Beach chairs/chaises
___ Hammock
___ Ground cloth/blanket
___ Sports gear: bicycles/tennis racket/balls/badminton set/Frisbee/swimming fins/kite/string
___ Fishing gear/tackle box
___ Picnic basket
___ Ice chest/cooler/thermos/ice packs/food containers
___ Raft/air mattress/repair kit/pump
___ Boat/oars
___ Life jackets/swimming aids: ear and noseplugs, goggles
___ Toys/games/books for children

Walking gear

___ Day pack/knapsack
___ Canteen
___ Compass
___ Pocket knife
___ Walking stick
___ Binoculars
___ Topographic maps/field books
___ Matches/waterproof container
___ Flashlight/batteries/bulbs
___ Rope/cord
___ Bottle opener

Men's Clothing

__ Underpants
__ T-shirts
__ Socks: sport/dress
__ Shirts
__ Pants: casual
__ Sport jacket
__ Polos/turtlenecks
__ Dungarees
__ Shorts
__ Sweaters/vests/down vest
__ Dress clothes
__ Belt/suspenders
__ Tie pin/jewelry/cuff links
__ Handkerchiefs
__ Pajamas
__ Robe
__ Sportswear: jogging suit/athletic supporter/sweat band/tennis outfit/sweat shirt/goggles
__ Bathing suit
__ Bathing suit top/robe
__ Bathing cap
__ Jacket/outerwear
__ Hat/cap/bandanas
__ Shoes: casual/sandals/dress
__ Boots/rubbers
__ Hiking boots
__ Sneakers
__ Slippers
__ Shower/beach shoes

Women's Clothing

__ Underpants
__ Brassieres/undershirts
__ Garter belt/garters/slip
__ Girdle
__ Stockings/panty hose/peds

___ Socks: sport
___ Blouses/tops
___ Skirts
___ Pants: casual
___ Polos/turtlenecks
___ Dungarees
___ Shorts
___ Halters
___ Sweaters/vest
___ Dress clothes
___ Belts/sashes
___ Jewelry
___ Handkerchiefs
___ Nightgowns/pajamas
___ Robe
___ Sportswear: jogging suit/sweat band/tennis outfit/ sweat shirt/goggles/running bra
___ Bathing suit
___ Bathing suit top/robe
___ Bathing cap
___ Jacket/outerwear
___ Raincoat
___ Hats
___ Scarves/bandanas
___ Pocketbook
___ Shoes: casual/sandals/dress
___ Boots/rubbers
___ Hiking boots
___ Sneakers
___ Slippers
___ Shower/beach shoes

Personal Effects and Toiletries

___ Toothbrush/toothpaste
___ Comb/brush
___ Barrettes/ribbons/rollers/clips/rubber bands/bobby pins
___ Hair dryer
___ Shower cap

- Wigs/wig box
- Shaving gear: razor/blades/shaving cream/brush/ aftershave lotion/electric razor/cord/styptic pencil
- Mirror
- Soap
- Shampoo
- Deodorant
- Skin lotions/creams/other toiletries/cleaners
- Perfumes/colognes
- Cosmetics: powder/rouge/lipstick/eye makeup/ eyelashes/lash curler
- Manicure/nail equipment
- Tweezer/scissors
- Bleaches/depilatories/hair coloring
- Suntan lotion/sunburn creams
- Lip balm
- Tissues/cotton balls/toilet tissues
- Cotton swabs
- Sanitary pads/belt/tampons
- Contraceptives
- Medical appliances: braces/trusses/elastic bandages
- Dentures/case/cleaner
- First-aid/kit/thermometer
- Aspirin/Dramamine
- Prescribed or other medications: antibiotics, antidiarrheal
- Toothpicks/dental floss
- Insect repellent

Accessories

- Suitcase/knapsack/day pack
- Wallet/money clip/pocketbook
- Money/traveler's checks/credit cards/checkbook
- Travel tickets
- IDs/licenses/medical insurance card/medical alert cards
- Date book/address book
- Diary/ledger book

___ Pens/paper/tape/scissors/typewriter/glue
___ Stationery/stamps
___ Work from office/home/correspondence/bills
___ Directions/reservation receipts
___ Watch
___ House lease
___ House keys
___ Eyeglasses/extra pair/eyeglass strap/lens cleaner
___ Contact lenses/cleaning equipment
___ Sunglasses/extra pair
___ Umbrella
___ Alarm clock
___ Travel iron
___ Camera/film/flash/film mailers
___ Sewing kit/shoe-polishing kit
___ Hangers
___ Laundry bag
___ Towels/washcloth/packaged wipes/beach towels
___ Hobbies: knitting/musical instruments
___ Books/cards/games/magazines
___ Personal items: pictures/teddy bear/good-luck charm
___ Maps/information for area
___ Radio/batteries
___ Tape recorder/tapes/earphones
___ Ax/hatchet
___ Equipment for pets
___ Liquor
___ Cigarettes/pipe gear/lighter
___ Boat/bike rack
___ List for repacking

SEE ALSO: BEFORE YOU GO (LIST 40) TRAVEL
ARRANGEMENTS (LIST 41) WHEN YOU RETURN (LIST 42)
OUTFITTING A RENTED VACATION HOME (LIST 53)
PACKING FOR A CAMPING TRIP (LIST 58) PACKING FOR
BACKPACKING (LIST 59) PREPARING/PACKING CAR FOR
A TRIP (LIST 60) PACKING FOR CANOE TRIP (LIST 63)
PACKING FOR INFANTS/YOUNG CHILDREN (LIST 64)

55. Packing for a Vacation at the Beach

This list, which was started twelve years ago when I first went to Cape Cod, was the catalyst for this book. It has everything you need for a comfortable vacation at the seashore or lakeside. It also includes items you need if the beach is in a foreign country. If you are going abroad, you certainly won't need every item mentioned, so adapt the list accordingly.

If you need household items, check Outfitting a Rented Vacation Home (list 53).

Beach Gear

— Beach towels
— Blankets/mats
— Beach bag/picnic basket
— Umbrella
— Beach chairs/chaises/pillows
— Hammock
— Rafts/air mattress/inner tubes
— Air pump
— Rubber boat/oars
— Life jackets/swimming aids: nose clips, goggles
— Surfboards
— Reflector
— Shields for eyes/nose/lips
— Thermos/ice chest
— Ice packs
— Food containers

Special Items for Children

— Night light

__ Favorite stuffed animal/blanket
__ Car games/car snacks
__ Toys/games
__ Pail/shovel
__ Beach toys/beach ball
__ Books

Men's Clothing

__ Underpants
__ T-shirts
__ Socks: sport/dress
__ Shirts
__ Pants: dress/casual
__ Sport jacket
__ Suit
__ Ties/ascot
__ Polos/turtlenecks
__ Dungarees
__ Shorts
__ Sweaters/vests
__ Belt/suspenders/garters
__ Tie pin/jewelry/cuff links
__ Handkerchiefs
__ Pajamas
__ Robe
__ Sportswear: jogging suit/athletic supporter/sweat band/tennis outfit/sweat shirt/goggles/sailing outfit
__ Bathing suit
__ Bathing suit top/beach robe/clothes to protect you from the sun
__ Bathing cap
__ Jacket/outerwear/lightweight jacket/windbreaker
__ Raincoat
__ Hat/cap/sun visor
__ Scarf
__ Shoes: dress/casual/sandals
__ Rain boots/rubbers
__ Sneakers/deck shoes

___ Slippers
___ Shower/beach shoes

Women's Clothing

___ Underpants
___ Brassieres/undershirts
___ Garter belt/garters
___ Girdle
___ Stockings/panty hose/peds
___ Socks: sport/dress
___ Slips
___ Blouses/tops
___ Skirts
___ Pants: dress/casual
___ Dresses
___ Polos/turtlenecks
___ Dungarees
___ Shorts
___ Halters
___ Sweaters/vests
___ Accessories: scarves
___ Belts/sashes
___ Jewelry
___ Handkerchiefs
___ Nightgowns/pajamas
___ Robe
___ Sportswear: jogging suit/sweat band/tennis outfit/ sweat shirt/goggles/sailing outfit/running bra
___ Bathing suits
___ Bathing suit top/beach robe/clothes to protect you from the sun
___ Bathing cap
___ Jacket/outerwear/lightweight jacket/windbreaker
___ Stole
___ Raincoat
___ Hats/sun hat/sun visor
___ Scarves/wraps
___ Pocketbook
___ Evening purse

___ Shoes: dress/casual/sandals
___ Rain boots/rubbers
___ Sneakers/deck shoes
___ Slippers
___ Shower/beach shoes

Personal Effects and Toiletries

___ Toothbrush/toothpaste
___ Comb/brush
___ Barrettes/ribbons/rollers/clips/rubber bands/bobby pins
___ Hair dryer
___ Shower cap
___ Wigs/wig box
___ Shaving gear: razor/blades/shaving cream/brush/after-shave lotion/electric razor/cord/styptic pencil
___ Soap
___ Shampoo
___ Deodorant
___ Skin lotion/creams/other toiletries/cleansers
___ Suntan lotion/sun screen/zinc oxide/after-sun moisturizer/sunburn cream
___ Perfumes/colognes
___ Cosmetics: Powder/rouge/lipstick/eye makeup/eyelashes/lash curler
___ Mirror
___ Manicure/nail equipment
___ Tweezer/scissors
___ Bleaches/depilatories/hair coloring
___ Lip balm
___ Calamine lotion
___ Insect repellent
___ Tissues/cotton balls/toilet tissues
___ Cotton swabs
___ Sanitary pads/belt/tampons
___ Contraceptives
___ Medical appliances: braces/trusses/elastic bandages
___ Dentures/denture container/denture cleaner
___ First-aid kit/thermometer

___ Aspirin/Dramamine
___ Special medications for heat problem: skin-rash cream
___ Prescribed or other medications
___ Toothpicks/dental floss
___ Spot-remover kit

Accessories

___ Suitcase/knapsack/day pack/beach bag
___ Wallet/money clip/pocketbook
___ Money/traveler's checks/credit cards/checkbook
___ Travel tickets
___ I.D.s/licenses/medical insurance cards/medical alert cards
___ Date book/address book
___ Diary/ledger books
___ Pens/paper/tape/glue
___ Briefcase/attaché case
___ Work from office/home/correspondence/typewriter
___ Directions/reservation receipts
___ Watch
___ House lease
___ House keys
___ Eyeglasses/extra pair/eyeglass strap/repair kit
___ Contact lenses/cleaning equipment
___ Sunglasses/extra pair
___ Folding knife
___ Umbrella
___ Calculator
___ Traveling clock/alarm
___ Travel iron
___ Camera/film/flash
___ Sewing kit
___ Repair kits: bicycle/car/raft
___ Shoe-shine equipment/shoetrees
___ Hangers
___ Laundry bag
___ Plastic bags (for wet clothes)
___ Towels/washcloth/packaged wipes/beach towels/mats

___ Sports gear: tennis racket/balls/fishing gear/Frisbee/ kite/bicycle/snorkel/goggles/fins/scuba gear/ear and nose plugs
___ Hobbies: knitting/musical instrument
___ Books/cards/games/magazines
___ Personal items: pictures/teddy bear/good-luck charm
___ Maps/information about area/compass
___ Flashlight/batteries
___ Radio/batteries
___ Tape recorder/tapes/earphones
___ Liquor
___ Cigarettes/pipe gear/lighter
___ Equipment for pets: litter box/special foods/food dish/ medicines/leash
___ Plants
___ Boat/bike rack
___ List for repacking

If Abroad

___ Passport/passport holder
___ Visas/IDs/international driver's license
___ Guidebooks/foreign-language books
___ Innoculations/vaccination certificate/translated medical alert forms
___ Currency converter
___ Currency for arrival in country of destination
___ Electricity converter
___ Special medications for going abroad: antidiarrheal, antibiotic

SEE ALSO: BEFORE YOU GO (LIST 40) TRAVEL
ARRANGEMENTS (LIST 41) WHEN YOU RETURN (LIST 42)
OUTFITTING A RENTED VACATION HOME (LIST 53)
PACKING FOR A DAY AT THE BEACH (LIST 56)
PREPARING/PACKING CAR FOR A TRIP (LIST 60)
PACKING FOR SAILING/BOATING (LIST 62) PACKING
FOR INFANTS/YOUNG CHILDREN (LIST 64)

56. Packing for a Day at the Beach

When we go to the beach, our decision on how much to take is based in part on how far we'll have to carry everything. One of our favorite spots on Cape Cod is about a mile from the parking lot. To there we carry only towels!

Preparations

— Check weather report
— Plan menu
— Shop for food
— Pack

Packing

— Beach bag/knapsack
— Blanket
— Beach towels
— Chairs/chaise/pillow
— Umbrella
— Reflector
— Suntan lotion/sun screen
— Nose/eye/lip guard
— Sunglasses/eyeglasses
— Sun hat/scarf
— Lip balm
— Insect repellent
— Shirt/cover-up against sun
— Wallet
— ID/beach permits/license

___ Keys
___ Money
___ Watch
___ Cosmetics/mirror
___ Comb/brush/barrettes/rubber bands/bobby pins
___ Cigarettes/lighter/matches/pipe gear
___ Paper/pencil/books/cards/games/magazines
___ Radio/tape recorder/tapes/earphones
___ Kite/ball/Frisbee/beach toys
___ Rafts/surfboard/scuba gear/snorkel/goggles/fins/life jackets
___ Bathing cap
___ Bathing suit/athletic supporter
___ Change of clothing
___ Sandals/beach shoes
___ Plastic bag (for wet clothes)
___ Ice chest/ice
___ Drinks/thermos/water jug
___ Bottle opener
___ Food/fruit
___ Plates
___ Silverware
___ Cups/glasses
___ Napkins
___ Knife/utensils
___ Food containers
___ Liquor
___ Garbage bags/fasteners
___ Toothpicks

SEE ALSO: PACKING FOR A PICNIC (LIST 57)

57. Packing for a Picnic

Preparations

__ Check weather report
__ Plan menu
__ Shop
__ Make dressing/sauces/marinades
__ Wash vegetables/fruit
__ Marinate meats
__ Cook foods: fry chicken, bake cupcakes
__ Pack

Basic Menu

__ Appetizer
__ Chips/pretzels
__ Main dish
__ Vegetables/salads
__ Bread
__ Mustard/ketchup/mayonnaise/butter
__ Salt/pepper/spices/dressings/sauces
__ Condiments: olives/pickles/relish
__ Drinks: alcoholic/nonalcoholic
__ Coffee/tea/cream/sugar
__ Desserts/fruits

Picnic gear

__ Basket
__ Tablecloth
__ Blanket/mats
__ Napkins
__ Plates

__ Silverware
__ Cups/glasses
__ Serving bowls
__ Food containers
__ Serving spoons
__ Sharp knife
__ Spatula/long-handled fork/tongs
__ Bottle opener/can opener
__ Thermos/jug
__ Ice chest/ice
__ Folding table
__ Chairs
__ Grill
__ Charcoal/wood
__ Lighter fluid/fire starter
__ Matches
__ Pots/pans/coffeepot
__ Pot holders
__ Apron
__ Paper towels/dishtowel
__ Plastic wrap/foil
__ Garbage bags
__ Scouring pad/soap/sponge
__ Packaged wipes
__ Toothpicks/dental floss

Personal Gear

__ Sunglasses/eyeglasses
__ Sun hat/scarf
__ Suntan lotion
__ Sweater/windbreaker
__ Sports equipment: fishing gear/ball/Frisbee
__ Camera/film
__ Radio/batteries/tape recorder/tapes/earphones
__ Insect repellent
__ Lantern/flashlight
__ Raingear/tarp
__ Cigarettes/lighter/pipe gear

- __ Day pack/pocketbook
- __ Wallet/IDs/licenses/medical alert cards/directions
- __ Money/credit cards
- __ Watch/house keys
- __ Books/magazines/cards/games
- __ Cosmetics/mirror
- __ Comb/brush

58. Packing for a Camping Trip

When we first wrote this list we thought about whether to add a tractor trailer as the last item. In fact, no one would ever take all of these items; pare the list down to meet your needs and your style.

Preparations

__ Make reservations at campground
__ Check on items provided by campground: picnic table, platform, grill, water/electricity, water, sewage
__ Check equipment
__ Practice setting up at home/count all parts
__ Clean cooking gear
__ Plan menu, including beverages
__ Shop for food, clothing, camping gear
__ Wash/dry salad items
__ Prepare salad dressings and barbeque sauces
__ Marinate meats/prepare precooked items

General Equipment

__ Tent
__ Tent poles/stakes
__ Patch kit
__ Ground cloths
__ Dining fly/tarps
__ Screen house
__ Dining table/card table
__ Chairs
__ Sleeping bags
__ Blanket/beach blanket
__ Foam pad/air mattresses/repair kit/air pump

— Cots
— Pillow/pillowcase
— Lantern/extra mantles
— Fuel for lantern
— Flashlight/extra batteries/bulbs
— Candles/citronella candles
— Shovel
— Ax/hatchet/folding saw
— Whetstone/sharpening stone
— Hammer/nails
— Rope/cord
— Clothesline/clothespins
— Small mat for cleaning feet outside tent
— Whisk broom/dust pan
— Portable toilet/plastic bags
— Toilet paper

Cooking Gear

— Stove
— Fuel for stove/funnel
— Oven
— Grill
— Wood/charcoal
— Matches/waterproof container
— Mess kit/pots/pans
— Coffeepot/filters
— Wire-handle kettle/tea strainer
— Long-handled utensils
— Skewers
— Pot holders
— Dishes/bowls
— Serving dishes
— Cups/glasses/mugs
— Silverware
— Utensils: vegetable peeler, serving spoon, colander
— Sharp knives
— Can opener

___ Bottle opener/corkscrew
___ Food containers
___ Juice container
___ Water jug
___ Thermos/canteen
___ Cooler/ice chest
___ Ice packs/ice
___ Dish pan
___ Dishtowels
___ Apron
___ Tablecloth
___ Napkins
___ Paper towels
___ Sponges
___ Biodegradable soap
___ Nylon scrubber/steel wool
___ Garbage bags/small plastic bags
___ Aluminum foil/plastic wrap
___ Spices/salt/pepper/sugar
___ Coffee/tea/hot chocolate
___ Condiments: mayonnaise/ketchup/mustard/relish
___ Bottled salad dressing/barbeque sauce
___ Food/drinks
___ Beer/liquor
___ Marshmallows/desserts/snacks

Accessories

___ Knapsack/suitcase
___ Money/traveler's checks/credit cards
___ Wallet/pocketbook
___ IDs/licenses/medical insurance cards/medical alert cards
___ Reservations/receipts
___ Maps/guidebooks/nature books
___ Compass
___ Day pack
___ Watch/traveling clock
___ House keys

___ Eyeglasses/extra pair/eyeglass strap/lens cleaner
___ Contact lenses/cleaning equipment
___ Sunglasses/extra pair
___ Cigarettes/pipe gear/lighter
___ Camera/film/flash/film mailers
___ Binoculars
___ Radio/batteries/earphones/tapes/tape recorder
___ Books/diary/magazines/pens/paper
___ Cards/games/toys
___ Sports gear: fishing equipment/license/Frisbee/ball
___ Hobbies: knitting/musical instruments
___ Sewing kit
___ Laundry bag
___ Fire arms/ammunition
___ Bow/arrow
___ Equipment for pets
___ Boat/bike rack
___ Emergency space blanket
___ List for repacking

Personal Effects and Toiletries

___ Toothbrush/toothpaste
___ Plastic drinking cup
___ Comb/brush
___ Barrettes/rollers/clips/rubber bands/bobby pins
___ Hair dryer
___ Shower cap
___ Shaving gear
___ Mirror
___ Soap/soap dish
___ Shampoo
___ Towels/washcloths/beach towels
___ Packaged wipes
___ Deodorant
___ Lotions/perfumes
___ Cosmetics
___ Nail equipment/manicure set

___ Tweezers/scissor
___ Lip balm
___ Tissues/cotton balls
___ Sanitary pads/belt/tampons
___ Contraceptives
___ Suntan lotion
___ Insect repellent
___ Calamine lotion
___ Medical appliances: braces, elastic bandage, trusses
___ Dentures/container/cleaner
___ First-aid kit/thermometer/snake-bite kit
___ Prescribed medications/aspirin
___ Toothpicks/dental floss
___ Extra laces for all shoes

Clothing

___ Underpants
___ T-shirts/brassieres/undershirts/slip
___ Girdle
___ Socks/stockings/peds
___ Pants/dungarees
___ Shorts
___ Shirts/polos
___ Halters
___ Dress clothes
___ Sweaters/down vest/sweat shirt
___ Belts/suspenders
___ Bandanas/handkerchiefs
___ Watch
___ Pajamas/nightgown
___ Robe
___ Sportswear: jogging suit/athletic supporter/tennis outfit/sweat pants/running bra
___ Bathing suit
___ Bathing cap
___ Beach robe
___ Lightweight jacket/heavy jacket
___ Rain gear: poncho/umbrella/boots

___ Hat/cap/scarves/gloves
___ Boots
___ Shoes/sneakers/sandals/moccasins
___ Slippers
___ Shower/beach shoes

SEE ALSO:
  BEFORE YOU GO (LIST 40)
  TRAVEL ARRANGEMENTS (LIST 41)
  WHEN YOU RETURN (LIST 42)
  PACKING FOR BACKPACKING (LIST 59)
  PREPARING/PACKING CAR FOR A TRIP (LIST 60)
  PACKING FOR INFANTS/YOUNG CHILDREN (LIST 64)
  WHAT TO HAVE IN A FIRST-AID KIT (LIST 81)

PACKING CHECK√ LISTS
Vacations

59. Packing for Backpacking

How much you take from this list clearly depends on how much weight you're willing to carry on your back. A good steak might be delicious at the end of the day, but the extra few pounds might make it not worth it. Most backpackers try to do it as lightly as possible.

Preparations

__ Decide on itinerary
__ Let people know itinerary, expected time of arrival
__ Make transportation arrangements
__ Make reservations if needed
__ Plan menus
__ Shop for food and gear
__ Check equipment
__ Pack

Equipment

__ Pack
__ Frame
__ Sleeping bag/straps
__ Pad/mattress
__ Tent/stakes
__ Tarp/tube tent
__ Ground sheet
__ Repair kit/rip-stop tape
__ Flashlight/batteries
__ Knife
__ Nylon cord
__ Canteen/water bottle/collapsible cup
__ Compass
__ Maps
__ Candles
__ Backpacking chair

Cooking Gear

___ Backpacking grill
___ Stove
___ Fuel
___ Cook kit: pans/pots/pot handle
___ Coffeepot
___ Long-handled utensils
___ Pot holders
___ Plate
___ Cup
___ Silverware
___ Screw-top jar
___ Can opener
___ Plastic bottle
___ Plastic bags/aluminum foil
___ Nylon scrubber
___ Biodegradable soap
___ Waterproof matches/container
___ Food/spices/salt/pepper

Personal Effects and Toiletries

___ Toothbrush/toothpaste
___ Comb/brush
___ Barrettes/rubber bands
___ Shaving gear
___ Mirror
___ Soap
___ Deodorant
___ Skin cream
___ Scissors/tweezers
___ Lip balm
___ Toilet paper/tissues
___ Sanitary belt/pads/tampons
___ Contraceptives
___ Medical appliances: braces/elastic bandages/trusses
___ Toothpicks/dental floss
___ Hand towel/washcloth

Medicines, First Aid, Safety

__ First-aid kit
__ Moleskin
__ Alcohol/foot powder
__ Sunburn lotion
__ Prescribed medications
__ Aspirin
__ Laxative/antidiarrheal
__ Iodine/water-purification tablets
__ Snake-bite kit
__ Insect repellent
__ Emergency/space blanket
__ Flares/whistle
__ Dimes for emergency phone calls
__ Small survival kit

Accessories

__ Money/traveler's checks/credit cards
__ IDs/licenses/medical insurance cards/medical alert cards
__ Travel tickets
__ Eyeglasses/extra pair/eyeglass strap/lens cleaner
__ Contact lenses/cleaning equipment
__ Sunglasses/extra pair
__ Diary/books
__ Paper/pencil
__ Watch
__ House keys
__ Lighter/cigarettes/pipe gear
__ Camera/film
__ Sewing kit/thimble
__ Fishing gear
__ Snow shoes/bindings
__ Cross-country skis/bindings/shoes/poles
__ Ice ax
__ Firearms/ammunition
__ Bow and arrow

Clothing

— Underpants
— T-shirts/brassieres
— Thermal underwear
— Socks: woolen/silk liners
— Shirts: polo/cotton
— Wool shirt
— Pants: dungarees/thermal/wool
— Shorts
— Sweater/down vest
— Money pouch/belt/suspenders
— Bandanas/handkerchief/sweat band
— Bathing suit/cap
— Jacket/parka
— Rain gear/gaiters
— Wool hat/sun hat
— Light wool gloves/mittens
— Boots
— Moccasins/sandals
— Lightweight shoes/sneakers
— Extra laces for all shoes

SEE ALSO:
  BEFORE YOU GO (LIST 40)
  TRAVEL ARRANGEMENTS (LIST 41)
  WHEN YOU RETURN (LIST 42)
  WHAT TO HAVE IN A FIRST-AID KIT (LIST 81)

60. Preparing/Packing Car for a Trip

This list is geared for the long car trip, and many items may be eliminated for a shorter trip.

Preparations

___ Buy travel and towing insurance
___ Plan itinerary/buy maps
___ Take car for tune-up
___ Get air conditioner checked
___ Have appropriate servicing for mileage
___ Get brakes, steering system, clutch, transmission, major systems checked.
___ Have car lubricated
___ Check signals/replace bulbs/buy fuses
___ Replace wiper blades
___ Buy tire-pressure gauge
___ Buy replacement parts that may be difficult to get: fan belt, plugs, wiper blades, hoses, special fluids, fuses
___ Attach side-view mirror
___ Wash/wax car
___ Wash windows, headlights, taillights
___ Empty ashtrays
___ Empty glove compartment of unnecessary items
___ Put maps, insurance card in glove compartment
___ Replace garbage bag
___ Empty trunk of unnecessary items
___ Check oil
___ Check water/replace antifreeze, coolant
___ Check water in battery
___ Check brake-fluid level
___ Refill windshield-washer fluid tank
___ Check tire pressure (including spare tire)
___ Check emergency gear: jack, lug wrench, tool kit
___ Fill up with gas, diesel fuel

___ Hook up trailers, hitches
___ Check electrical connections on directional signals for trailers, hitches
___ Put on bike rack, ski rack, luggage rack
___ Get change for tolls
___ Pack car, trunk

Packing

___ Spare tire
___ Jack/lug wrench/wedges
___ Tire-pressure gauge
___ Air pump
___ Flares/white flag
___ Flashlight/extra batteries
___ Jumper cables
___ Gas can/water can
___ Extra oil/oil spout/lubricating oil
___ Spare parts: fan belt/plugs/wiper blades/hoses/ special fluids/fuses
___ Tool kit/rags
___ Rope/elastic tie cords
___ Window cleaner/paper towels
___ Garbage bags/sickness bags
___ Whisk broom
___ Seat cushion/back support
___ Air freshener
___ First-aid kit/Dramamine
___ Jug of drinking water

For Rough Driving

___ Window scraper
___ Chains/snow tires
___ Shovel
___ Sand/rock salt
___ De-icer
___ Dry gas
___ Tow chain
___ Emergency blanket

Important Papers

___ Registration
___ License
___ Insurance card/phone numbers of insurance offices
___ Towing cards
___ Gasoline credit cards
___ Car repair manual
___ List of dealers/service centers
___ IDs
___ Maps/directions
___ Reservation receipts

Personal Gear

___ Eyeglasses/extra glasses/sunglasses
___ Driving gloves
___ Extra keys/magnetic key box
___ Toll-booth change
___ Pocketbook/wallet
___ Cassettes/tapes
___ Portable radio/batteries
___ Tissues
___ Toiletry kit/towel/packaged wipes
___ Books
___ Pen/paper
___ Cigarettes/lighter/pipe gear
___ Car games
___ Pillow
___ Blanket
___ Umbrella/rain gear
___ Matches
___ Snacks
___ Thermos
___ Necessary clothing
___ Suitcase/knapsack

SEE ALSO: CAR CARE (LIST 38)   BEFORE YOU GO (LIST 40)
   TRAVEL ARRANGEMENTS (LIST 41)   WHEN YOU RETURN
   (LIST 42)

61. Packing for a Bike Trip

What you take will depend on where you're cycling to, for how long, what the weather will be, accessabil- ity of stores and laundromats, and the strength of your legs. Some people send food packages ahead so they don't have to carry it all with them. If you're traveling in a group, you can divide up the camping equipment among you.

If you are traveling abroad and own a foreign cycle, you might want to bring your sales slip so that you are not charged duty when reentering the United States.

Preparations

__ Plan itinerary/get maps/speak to friends about their experiences/get information about area to be visited
__ Call biking groups, hostels, hotels for information and passes
__ Make reservations
__ Send deposits
__ Call airlines, trains, buses about regulations for shipping bike
__ Buy tickets
__ Get passports, visas, vaccinations
__ Get traveler's checks, exchange currency
__ Leave traveler's-check numbers with relative or friend
__ Put ID number permanently on bike
__ Test equipment
__ Make list of brand name, model of bike, frame size, spoke length, free wheel brand, cotterless crank
__ Coat seams of tent and rain gear with sealer
__ Plug handlebar ends/retape handlebars
__ Replace worn parts: brake pads/straps/pedal pads/ reflectors
__ Buy needed items

___ Pack
___ Pack bike/test weight distribution
___ Confirm tickets, travel reservations

For Carrying

___ Bicycle
___ Saddle cover/bike cover/large plastic bags to cover saddlebags/sleeping bag
___ Saddlebags
___ Rear cycle bag
___ Front cycle bag
___ Rear luggage carrier
___ Day pack
___ Elastic cords

For Tires

___ Pump/pump clips
___ Extra tires/tubes/valves
___ Tire savers
___ Patch kit
___ Pressure gauge
___ Tire irons
___ Tire valve tightener

Tools and Spare Parts

___ Wrench/cone wrench
___ Allen wrench/spoke wrench
___ Small locking pliers
___ Cotter pins
___ Cotterless crank tools
___ Nuts/bolts to fit bike
___ Extra nuts/bolts for carrier
___ Specialized tools for your bike model
___ Metal file
___ Extra brake block with shoes
___ Rear brake cable

— Rear gear cable
— Spare temporary axle
— Spray lubricant
— Free wheel extractor
— Chain tool
— Extra spokes with nipples
— Handlebar tape/electrician's tape/wire/wire cutters
— Bicycle repair book

For Safety

— Front light/extra batteries/bulbs
— Rear reflector
— Rearview mirror
— Helmet
— Safety vest/orange tape/leg lights
— Goggles
— Flag
— Bell/whistle/horn
— Lock/chain/cable
— Pants clips
— Safety spacer
— Space blanket
— Dog repellent

Miscellaneous

— Water bottle/clips
— Cyclometer
— Toe clips/straps
— Compass

Camping

— Tent/poles/stakes
— Rope/nylon cord
— Nylon tarp/dining fly/ground cloth
— Repair tape for nylon
— Sleeping bag/stuff sack/sleeping-bag straps

___ Foam pad/air mattress
___ Sheets/sleeping sack
___ Pillow
___ Stove/fuel/funnel
___ Pots/frying pan/cook kit/cooking utensils
___ Dishes/cups/silverware
___ Knife
___ Food containers/egg case
___ Food tubes
___ Plastic bottles
___ Can opener
___ Pot holder
___ Matches/waterprooof container
___ Plastic scouring pad/soap dish
___ Dishtowel
___ Toilet paper
___ Flashlight/extra batteries/bulbs
___ Candles
___ Water-purification tablets
___ Small garbage bags

Personal Effects and Toiletries

___ Rubberized toiletry bag
___ Toothbrush/toothpaste
___ Comb/brush
___ Barrettes/clips/rubber bands
___ Shaving gear: razor/blades/shaving cream
___ Soap/soap dish
___ Shampoo
___ Deodorant
___ Skin lotion/creams/cleansers
___ Suntan lotion
___ Cosmetics: powder/rouge/lipstick/eye makeup
___ Small mirror
___ Tweezers/scissors
___ Lip balm
___ Tissues
___ Cotton swabs

- ___ Sanitary pads/belts/tampons
- ___ Contraceptives
- ___ Medical appliances: braces/trusses/dentures/elastic bandages
- ___ First-aid kit
- ___ Aspirin/Dramamine
- ___ Prescribed or other medications
- ___ Toothpicks/dental floss
- ___ Foot-care materials: clippers/corn pads/foot spray and powder
- ___ Insect repellent

Accessories

- ___ Wallet/money clip/money belt
- ___ Money/traveler's checks/credit cards/checkbook
- ___ Travel tickets
- ___ IDs/licenses/passport/visa/medical insurance cards/ medical alert cards
- ___ Address book/diary
- ___ Pens/paper
- ___ Directions/reservation receipts/guidebooks
- ___ Maps/map case
- ___ Watch
- ___ House keys
- ___ Eyeglasses/extra pair/eyeglass strap/lens cleaner
- ___ Contact lenses/cleaning equipment
- ___ Sunglasses/extra pair
- ___ Cigarettes/lighter/pipe gear
- ___ Travel alarm clock
- ___ Camera/film
- ___ Sewing kit
- ___ Laundry bag
- ___ Plastic bags (for wet clothes/garbage)
- ___ Towels/washcloth/packaged wipes
- ___ Sports gear: Frisbee/fishing gear/binoculars
- ___ Pocket knife
- ___ Hobbies: knitting/musical instrument
- ___ Books/cards/games/magazines

___ Blueprint/packing list
___ Tape recorder/tapes/earphones/radio
___ Extra laces for all shoes

Clothing

___ Underpants
___ T-shirts/undershirts/brassieres/halters
___ Thermal underwear
___ Socks: sport/wool/peds
___ Polos/turtlenecks
___ Long-sleeve wool shirt
___ Dungarees
___ Dress outfit
___ Shorts: cycling/regular
___ Cycling tights
___ Sweaters/down vest
___ Belt/suspenders/jewelry/accessories
___ Handkerchiefs/bandanas
___ Pajamas/nightgown
___ Bathing suit/bathing cap
___ Jacket/outerwear/sweat shirt
___ Raincoat/rain pants/rain hat
___ Sun hat/wool hat/scarf
___ Cycling gloves
___ Sweat band
___ Walking boots
___ Cycling shoes
___ Sandals/moccasins
___ Rain boots/rubbers
___ Shower/beach shoes

SEE ALSO: BEFORE YOU GO (LIST 40) TRAVEL
ARRANGEMENTS (LIST 41) WHEN YOU RETURN (LIST 42)
WHAT TO HAVE IN A FIRST-AID KIT (LIST 81)

62. Packing for Sailing/ Boating

The duration of your trip, the weather, the type of sailing or boating you're doing, and your destination will all be factors in determining what you pack. We suggest you check on what's available in the ports where you'll be stopping.

Carefully assess your boating skills and, if necessary, hire an experienced crew or pair yourself with an experienced sailor. For safety's sake, let others know your destination, course, and anticipated date of arrival.

Clothing

___ Underpants
___ T-shirts/brassieres/undershirts
___ Long underwear
___ Garter belt/garters/girdle/slip
___ Wool and cotton socks/stockings/peds
___ Shirts/blouses/halters
___ Polos/turtlenecks/jerseys
___ Pants/dungarees/wool pants
___ Shorts
___ Skirts
___ Dress clothes for shore: blazer, tie, dress, stole
___ Wool sweaters/sweat shirts/down vest
___ Bandanas/scarves/handkerchiefs
___ Jewelry/belts/accessories
___ Nightgown/pajamas/robe
___ Sportswear: tennis outfit/jogging suit/athletic supporter/sweat bands/skindiving and snorkeling gear
___ Bathing suit/bathing suit cover-up/bathing cap

___ Wool jacket
___ Windbreaker
___ Wool cap/sun hat
___ Leather gloves/sailing gloves/wool gloves/rubber gloves
___ Leather moccasins/rubber deck shoes/sandals/sneakers/shower shoes/casual shoes/dress shoes/extra shoelaces

For Foul Weather

___ Southwester
___ Rain jacket
___ Rain trouser/suspenders
___ Sea boots
___ Knitted wristlets/silk scarf
___ Waterproof mittens
___ Towels for around neck

Personal Effects and Toiletries

___ Toothpaste/toothbrush
___ Comb/brush
___ Barrettes/ribbons/rollers/clips/rubber bands/bobby pins
___ Hair dryer
___ Shower cap
___ Wigs/wig box
___ Shaving gear: razor blades/shaving cream/brush/after-shave lotion/electric razor/cord/styptic pencil
___ Soap
___ Shampoo
___ Deodorant
___ Skin lotions/creams/other toiletries/cleansers
___ Perfumes/colognes
___ Cosmetics: powder/rouge/lipstick/eye makeup/eyelashes/lash curler
___ Mirror
___ Manicure and nail equipment
___ Tweezers/scissors
___ Bleaches/depilatories/hair coloring

___ Lip balm
___ Tissues/cotton balls/toilet tissues
___ Cotton swabs
___ Sanitary pads/belt/tampons
___ Contraceptives
___ Medical appliances: braces/trusses/elastic bandages
___ Dentures/containers/denture cleaner
___ First-aid kit/thermometer
___ Aspirin/Dramamine
___ Prescribed or other medication: laxative, antidiarrheal, toothache remedies, eye wash
___ Toothpicks/dental floss
___ Foot powder/moleskin

Accessories

___ Suitcase/knapsack
___ Wallet/money clip/pocketbook
___ Money/traveler's checks/credit cards/checkbook
___ IDs/licenses/medical insurance cards/medical alert cards
___ Travel tickets/reservation receipts
___ Date book/address book
___ Diary/ledger books/ship's log
___ Pens/paper
___ Waterproof/ditty bag
___ Waterproof cases/containers
___ Work from office/home/correspondence
___ Charts/maps/sailing books/tables
___ Waterproof watch
___ House keys
___ Eyeglasses/extra pair/eyeglass strap/lens cleaner
___ Contact lenses/cleaning equipment
___ Sunglasses/extra pair
___ Binoculars
___ Calculator
___ Traveling clock/alarm
___ Travel iron
___ Camera/film/waterproof case

__ Sewing kit
__ Shoe-shine equipment/shoetrees
__ Hangers/clothespins/clothes hammock
__ Laundry bag
__ Plastic bags (for wet clothes)
__ Towels/washcloth
__ Sports gear: tennis racket/balls/Frisbee/fishing gear
__ Hobbies: knitting/musical instrument
__ Books/cards/games/magazines
__ Personal items: pictures, teddy bear, good-luck charm
__ Maps/information about area/cruising guides
__ Radio/batteries
__ Tape recorder/tapes/earphones
__ Cigarettes/pipe gear/lighter/extra flints
__ Liquor
__ Equipment for pets
__ Shopping bags/string bags
__ List for repacking

For Abroad

__ Foreign-language dictionaries/guides
__ Money converter
__ Passports/visa
__ Vaccination certificates
__ Items for trading
__ Electricity converter

SEE ALSO: BEFORE YOU GO (LIST 40) TRAVEL
ARRANGEMENTS (LIST 41) WHEN YOU RETURN (LIST 42)
PUTTING A BOAT IN THE WATER (LIST 48) PACKING FOR
A TRIP ABROAD (LIST 51) WHAT TO HAVE IN A FIRST-AID
KIT (LIST 81)

63. Packing for a Canoe Trip

Could all this possibly fit in a canoe without sinking it? We doubt it. However, we assume that either you'll leave the camping equipment and clothing on shore; that you're in a group with several canoes; or that you'll be scaling the list down to more reasonable proportions.

The list includes equipment for both white water and lake canoeing. Consider which equipment is applicable for your trip.

For Canoeing

__ Canoe
__ Paddles/spare paddle
__ Canoe poles
__ Extra flotation for canoe
__ Cushions/kneepads
__ Floor mats
__ Seats/swivel seat/camp chairs
__ Outboard motor/motor bracket
__ Gas can/fuel
__ Spare parts for motor/tools
__ Bailer/large sponge
__ Portage yoke
__ Tie downs
__ Nylon line
__ Heavy rope/throw rope
__ Painters
__ Caribiner/clips
__ Winch
__ Duct tape/wire
__ Canoe repair kit/rubber cement
__ Large rucksacks/waterproof liners/pack baskets

___ Day pack
___ Life jackets/flotation vests
___ Helmets
___ Compass/maps/waterproof case
___ Canteen/thermos

For Camping

___ Tent
___ Tent poles/stakes
___ Ground sheet/tarp/rain fly
___ Sleeping bags
___ Sleeping pad/air mattress/air pump/repair kit for air mattress/hammock
___ Pillow/pillowcase
___ Mosquito netting
___ Lantern/extra mantles/fuel
___ Flashlight/batteries/bulbs
___ Candles
___ Rope/cord/twine
___ Shovel
___ Ax/folding saw
___ Whetstone file/sharpening stone

For Cooking

___ Stove/fuel/funnel
___ Oven
___ Grill
___ Ice chest
___ Cook kit/pots/pans/pot handle
___ Coffeepot
___ Long-handled utensils
___ Pot holders
___ Plates/bowls
___ Cups
___ Silverware
___ Sharp knife
___ Can opener/corkscrew/bottle opener

___ Water jug
___ Plastic containers for food, juice
___ Aluminum foil/plastic bags/garbage bags
___ Scouring pad/sponge
___ Biodegradable soap
___ Dishtowels
___ Paper towels/napkins
___ Food/spices/staples
___ Toothpicks/dental floss
___ Matches/waterproof container/fire ribbon/butane
    lighter

Personal Effects and Toiletries

___ Toothbrush/toothpaste
___ Comb/brush
___ Barrettes/rubber bands
___ Shaving gear
___ Mirror
___ Germicidal soap (biodegradable)
___ Deodorant
___ Skin lotion
___ Cosmetics
___ Scissors/tweezers
___ Lip balm
___ Toilet paper/tissues
___ Sanitary pads/belt/tampons
___ Contraceptives
___ Suntan lotion/sunburn cream
___ Insect repellent/head net
___ Medical appliances: braces/elastic bandage/dentures/
    trusses
___ Towels/washcloth

Medicines/First Aid/Safety

___ First-aid kit
___ Moleskin
___ Prescribed or other medications

___ Aspirin
___ Iodine/water-purification tablets
___ Snake-bite kit
___ Emergency/space blanket
___ Emergency water supply/food supply
___ Whistle/flares/smoke bombs

Accessories

___ Knapsack/day pack
___ Money/traveler's checks/credit cards
___ Money pouch/wallet
___ IDs/licenses/medical insurance cards/medical alert cards/reservation receipts
___ Eyeglasses/extra pair/eyeglass strap/lens cleaner
___ Contact lenses/cleaning equipment
___ Sunglasses/extra pair
___ Watch
___ Two sets of house keys (each to be carried by different people)
___ Pocket knife
___ Guidebooks/books/diary
___ Pencils/paper
___ Binoculars
___ Camera/film
___ Waterproof cases
___ Sewing kit/safety pins/thimble
___ Hobbies: knitting/musical instrument
___ Cards/games
___ Radio/battery/earphones
___ Liquor
___ Cigarettes/pipe gear/lighter
___ Fishing gear
___ Firearms/ammunition
___ Bow/arrow
___ Boat rack

Clothing

___ Underpants

___ T-shirts/brassieres
___ Long underwear
___ Socks
___ Shirts/polos
___ Pants/dungarees
___ Shorts
___ Halters
___ Bathing suit
___ Bathing cap
___ Belts/suspenders
___ Sweaters/down vest
___ Outer jacket/windbreaker
___ Bandanas/handkerchiefs/sweat band
___ Sun hat/wool hat
___ Rain wear/wet suit
___ Sneakers/moccasins
___ Rubber-bottom boots
___ River shoes/wet-suit booties
___ Gloves
___ Extra shoelaces

SEE ALSO:

PACKING FOR A CAMPING TRIP (LIST 58)
PREPARING/PACKING A CAR FOR A TRIP (LIST 60)
WHAT TO HAVE IN A FIRST-AID KIT (LIST 81)

PACKING CHECK √ LISTS
Vacations

64. Packing for Infants/ Young Children

Recently a friend, her husband, and their fourteen-month-old baby packed for a European trip. She filled one suitcase for herself and her husband and three suitcases for the baby. Laundry services are often a critical issue when traveling with young children, and quantity should be based on how frequently you believe you'll be able to get a wash done.

Preparations

___ Check with place you are going to about equipment, babysitting services, and laundry services

For Sleeping

___ Crib/bassinette/cradle
___ Sheets
___ Blankets/pillow
___ Waterproof sheet
___ Blanket clips
___ Mosquito netting
___ Crib bumpers

For Eating

___ Highchair/booster seat
___ Heating tray/foods
___ Food grinder
___ Spoon
___ Bibs
___ Bottles/nipples
___ Formula

___ Bottle brush/nipple brush
___ Bottle caps
___ Sterlizing equipment
___ Bottle warmer
___ Breast-feeding pads/diaper for burping
___ Plastic containers for food
___ Packaged wipes/washcloth
___ Paper towels

For Transporting

___ Carriage/stroller
___ Car seat
___ Backpack/front carrier
___ Carriage strap

For Cleaning and Changing

___ Disposable diapers/diapers/rubber pants
___ Pre-moistened wipes
___ Lotion
___ Powder
___ Soap
___ Shampoo
___ Bathtub
___ Towel/washcloth
___ Plastic bags with ties
___ Nail clippers
___ Cotton balls with container

For Playing

___ Playpen
___ Toys/games/books
___ Favorite animal/favorite object
___ Pacifier
___ Mobiles

Clothing

___ Undershirts/diapers/rubber pants
___ Socks
___ Stretch suits/kimonos/overalls/shirts
___ Dress clothes
___ Sweaters/hats/mittens
___ Shoes/shoe polish/booties
___ Jacket/snowsuit/bunting

Miscellaneous

___ Suitcase
___ Carry bag
___ Medications/vitamins/thermometer
___ Insect repellent
___ Special medical equipment: vaporizer
___ Toilet seat
___ Night light
___ Luggage rack

In Diaper Bag for Short Trips

___ Disposable diapers
___ Pre-moistened wipes
___ Wash cloth
___ Plastic bag
___ Change of clothing
___ Bottle
___ Food
___ Snack
___ Toys
___ Pacifier

65. Packing/Sending Children to Camp

Preparations

__ Order nametags
__ Check camp instructions/find out what's needed: linens, overnight camping gear
__ Check if trunk has to be sent ahead of time/arrange shipping
__ Buy required items, uniforms
__ Sew labels/print names on everything
__ Find out frequency of laundry service
__ Get medical examinations, innoculations
__ Fill necessary prescriptions
__ Get dental checkup
__ Check eyeglasses
__ Arrange transportation to and from camp
__ Send instructions to camp: special medications, diets, activity restrictions
__ Notify camp where you can be reached
__ Duplicate trunk key/send to camp
__ Get trunk and duffle bag ready/label with name and address
__ Note visiting day on calendar/arrange for visitor if you will be out of town
__ Discuss child's feelings, concerns, expectations
__ Discuss what child wants in care packages, requests for visiting day
__ Go over letter writing with child
__ Send letters to children before departure so that they are waiting when children arrive

__ Mail care package
__ Pack lunch for trip
__ Take directions and travel instructions

Clothing

(Some camps suggest you send old clothing, since many items are lost during the summer.)

__ Underpants
__ T-shirts/undershirts/brassieres/slip
__ Socks/stockings/peds
__ Shorts
__ Pants/dungarees
__ Short-sleeve shirts/polos
__ Long-sleeve shirts/polos
__ Halters
__ Camp uniforms
__ Sweat shirts/sweaters/down vest
__ Dress clothes
__ Lightweight jacket
__ Heavy jacket
__ Bathing suits
__ Bathing cap
__ Beach robe
__ Sportswear: jogging suit/tennis outfit/goggles/sweat band/riding outfit/running bra
__ Pajamas: warm/lightweight
__ Bathrobe
__ Belts/suspenders
__ Handkerchief/bandanas
__ Hat/cap/scarves
__ Raincoat/poncho/umbrella
__ Rubber boots
__ Shoes/hiking boots/sneakers/dress shoes
__ Slippers
__ Beach shoes/thongs
__ Extra shoelaces

Linens

___ Towels/washcloths
___ Sheets/pillowcases
___ Blankets
___ Sleeping bag/ground cloth
___ Pillow
___ Laundry bag/plastic bags

Accessories

___ Suitcase/trunk/duffle bag
___ Change for canteen/money/wallet/medical alert tags
___ Address book
___ Books/comics/diary
___ Stationery/pens/pencils
___ Addressed envelopes/postcards
___ Stamps
___ Watch/clock
___ Jewelry
___ Eyeglasses/extra pair/eyeglass strap/lens cleaner
___ Contact lenses/cleaning equipment
___ Sunglasses/extra pair
___ Camera/film/flash/film mailers
___ Cards/games/jacks/balls/radio/batteries/earphones
___ Stuffed animals/special toys/family pictures
___ Sports gear: fishing pole/tennis racket/Frisbee/ baseball mitt
___ Hobbies: musical instruments
___ Binoculars
___ Backpack
___ Canteen/mess kit
___ Pocket knife
___ Compass
___ Flashlight/batteries/extra bulb
___ Sewing kit
___ Hangers
___ Travel iron
___ Travel tickets
___ Packing list taped to trunk hood for repacking

Personal Effects and Toiletries

__ Toothbrush/toothpaste
__ Plastic drinking cup
__ Brush/comb
__ Hair clips/barrettes/rubber bands/bobby pins
__ Hair dryer
__ Soap/soap dish
__ Shampoo
__ Shower cap
__ Deodorant
__ Skin lotion/perfumes
__ Suntan lotion
__ Lip balm
__ Tissues/cotton swabs
__ Calamine lotion
__ Insect repellent
__ Medication (give to camp staff with instructions)
__ Dental brace/medical appliances

For Adolescents

__ Makeup
__ Shaving gear
__ Mirror
__ Tweezers/scissors
__ Manicure/nail equipment
__ Bleaches/depilatories
__ Sanitary pads/belt/tampons

SEE ALSO:
TRAVEL ARRANGEMENTS (LIST 41)
PREPARING/PACKING A CAR FOR A TRIP (LIST 60)

66. Packing/Sending Children to College/Boarding School

Some students may prefer packing everything they may need for the entire year. Others may prefer taking fall and winter clothes first, spring and summer items later on during the year. Your proximity to the school may affect your decision.

If possible, you should visit the school, see your room and decide on what you'll need. If not, you might want to check with the school about what's needed.

If you are going to school far away, you may want to send a trunk prior to your departure so that it will be there when you arrive.

Preparations

— Read instructions from school
— Sign up for dormitory room/find apartment/rent room
— Make list of items the school provides for the room
— Make shopping list of needed items/shop
— Decide if trunk is to be sent ahead of time
— Make appointment for physical checkup
— Make appointment for dental checkup
— Have eyes examined/have extra glasses made
— Change address on subscriptions
— Have mail forwarded
— Open bank accounts near school
— Arrange for phone installation
— Arrange meal plans
— Arrange transportation
— Pack

For Studying

__ Typewriter
__ Desk lamp/bed lamp
__ Wastebasket
__ Calculator
__ Dictionary
__ Books: pleasure reading/reference (thesaurus, desk encyclopedia)
__ Pens/pencils/ruler
__ Stationery/stamps
__ Book bag/briefcase/knapsack
__ Scissors/tape/paper clips/glue
__ Stapler/staples
__ Desk organizer/blotter
__ Pencil sharpener

For Pleasure

__ Radio/batteries
__ Television
__ Stereo/headphones/speakers/speaker wire
__ Alarm clock/clock radio
__ Camera/film/flash/mailers
__ Tape recorder/tapes/cassettes
__ Records
__ Cards/games/poker chips
__ Hobbies: knitting/collections
__ Musical instruments
__ Sports gear: tennis racket/skis/ice skates/roller skates/Frisbee
__ Bicycle
__ Favorite stuffed animal/good-luck charm
__ Photo album/family pictures

For Room

__ Posters/pictures
__ Plants/plant stand
__ Curtains

___ Rug
___ Throw pillows
___ Furniture
___ Vase
___ Ashtrays
___ Sheets
___ Mattress pad
___ Pillowcases
___ Pillow
___ Blankets
___ Bedspread
___ Towels/washcloths
___ Bath mat
___ Laundry bag
___ Hot plate
___ Coffeepot/pots
___ Mugs/glasses
___ Soup bowl/dishes
___ Silverware
___ Bottle opener
___ Night light

Accessories

___ Suitcase/knapsack/trunk
___ Wallet/money clip/pocketbook
___ Money/traveler's checks/credit cards/checkbook/
bankbook
___ Travel tickets
___ IDs/licenses/medical insurance cards/medical alert
cards
___ Papers from college for registration/financial aid/
orientation
___ Maps/information about area/directions
___ Date book/address book
___ Diary/ledger book
___ Overnight bag/day pack
___ Watch
___ House keys/key chain

___ Eyeglasses/extra pair/eyeglass strap/lens cleaner
___ Contact lenses/cleaning equipment
___ Sunglasses/extra pair
___ Lighter/cigarettes/pipe gear
___ Jewelry box
___ Iron
___ Sewing kit
___ Flashlight
___ Shoe-shine equipment/shoetrees/shoe bag/laces
___ Spot remover
___ Cleaning equipment: sponges/duster/broom
___ Small tool kit
___ Pictures hooks/thumb tacks
___ Hangers/garment bags
___ List for repacking

Personal Effects and Toiletries

___ Toothbrush/toothpaste
___ Drinking cup
___ Comb/brush
___ Barrettes/ribbons/rollers/clips/rubber bands/bobby pins
___ Hair dryer
___ Shower cap
___ Shaving gear: razor/blades/shaving cream/brush/ aftershave lotion/electric razor/cord/styptic pencil
___ Soap/soap dish
___ Shampoo
___ Deodorant
___ Skin lotion/creams/other toiletries/cleansers
___ Perfumes/colognes
___ Cosmetics: powder/rouge/lipstick/eye makeup/ eyelashes/lash curler
___ Manicure/nail equipment
___ Tweezer/scissors
___ Bleaches/depilatories/hair coloring
___ Lip balm
___ Tissues/cotton balls/toilet tissues

— Cotton swabs
— Sanitary pads/belt/tampons
— Medical appliances: braces/trusses/elastic bandages
— First-aid kit/thermometer
— Aspirin/vitamins
— Prescribed or other medications
— Toothpicks/dental floss
— Mirror
— Insect repellent
— Toiletries bag
— Extra shoelaces

Boys' Clothing

— Underpants
— T-shirts
— Socks: sport/dress
— Shirts
— Pants: dress/casual
— Sport jacket
— Suit
— Uniform
— Evening clothes: tuxedo
— Ties/ascot
— Polos/turtlenecks
— Dungarees
— Shorts
— Sweater/vests
— Belt/suspenders/garters
— Tie pin/jewelry/cuff links
— Handkerchiefs
— Pajamas
— Robe
— Sportswear: jogging suit/athletic supporter/sweat band/tennis outfit/sweat shirt/goggles
— Bathing suit
— Bathing suit top/robe
— Bathing cap
— Jacket/outerwear

__ Overcoat
__ Raincoat/umbrella
__ Hat/cap
__ Scarf/muffler
__ Gloves
__ Shoes: dress/casual/sandals
__ Boots/rubbers
__ Sneakers
__ Slippers
__ Shower/beach shoes

Girls' Clothing

__ Underpants
__ Brassieres/undershirts
__ Garter belt/garters
__ Girdle/slip
__ Stockings/panty hose/peds
__ Socks: sport/dress
__ Slips
__ Blouses/tops
__ Skirts
__ Pants: dress/casual
__ Dresses
__ Suits
__ Uniform
__ Evening clothes: gowns
__ Polos/turtlenecks
__ Dungarees
__ Shorts
__ Halters
__ Sweaters/vests
__ Accessories: scarves
__ Belts/sashes
__ Jewelry
__ Handkerchiefs
__ Nightgowns/pajamas
__ Robe

___ Sportswear: jogging suit/sweat band/tennis outfit/ sweat shirt/goggles/running bra
___ Bathing suit
___ Bathing suit top/robe
___ Bathing cap
___ Jacket/outerwear
___ Overcoat/stole
___ Raincoat/umbrella
___ Hats
___ Scarves/wraps
___ Gloves
___ Pocketbook
___ Evening purse
___ Shoes: dress/casual/sandals
___ Boots/rubbers
___ Sneakers
___ Slippers
___ Shower/beach shoes

SEE ALSO:
  TRAVEL ARRANGEMENTS (LIST 41)
  PREPARING/PACKING A CAR FOR A TRIP (LIST 60)

67. Packing for a Business Trip

The clothes in this list fall into two sections: basic items (those needed purely for business) and optional items (for those who mix pleasure with business). In figuring quantity, consider whether you'll wear one outfit during the day and another for your evening appointments.

Preparations

___ Plan itinerary
___ Get passport and visas
___ Make copy of itinerary for associates, secretary, spouse
___ Confirm tickets, hotel reservations, car rental, travel arrangements
___ Make list of people to be seen/get correct spelling and pronunciation of names and times of appointments
___ Confirm business appointments
___ Organize business papers for trip/make list of items needed for each appointment
___ Buy necessary gifts for host and hostess
___ Have clothes cleaned, shoes shined
___ Check supplies: tapes for tape recorder, batteries for calculator
___ Organize/prepare audiovisual aids
___ Prepare material, documents for meetings
___ Prepare lectures, presentations
___ Arrange transportation to airport
___ Leave instructions how to handle affairs during your absence/arrange coverage
___ Leave emergency numbers
___ Finish outstanding correspondence and business prior to departure

__ Get traveler's checks, money, foreign currency
__ Pack business papers
__ Pack clothing

Basic Men's Clothing

__ Underpants
__ T-shirts
__ Socks: sports/dress
__ Shirts
__ Pants: dress
__ Sports jacket
__ Suit
__ Ties
__ Belt/suspenders/garters
__ Tie pin/jewelry/cuff links
__ Handkerchiefs
__ Pajamas
__ Robe
__ Overcoat
__ Raincoat
__ Hat/cap
__ Scarf/muffler
__ Gloves
__ Shoes: dress
__ Slippers

Optional Men's Clothing

__ Sport socks
__ Evening clothes: tuxedo
__ Ascot
__ Polos/turtlenecks
__ Casual pants
__ Dungarees
__ Shorts
__ Sweaters/vest
__ Sportswear: jogging suit/athletic supporter/sweat band/tennis outfit/sweat shirt/goggles

Miscellaneous

__ Bathing suit
__ Bathing suit top/robe
__ Bathing cap
__ Jacket/outerwear
__ Casual shoes/sandals
__ Sneakers
__ Boots/rubbers
__ Shower/beach shoes

Basic Women's Clothing

__ Underpants
__ Brassieres/undershirts
__ Garter belt/garters
__ Girdle
__ Stockings/panty hose/peds
__ Slips
__ Blouses/tops
__ Shirts
__ Dresses
__ Suits
__ Accessories: scarves
__ Belts/sashes
__ Jewelry
__ Handkerchiefs
__ Nightgown/pajamas
__ Robe
__ Overcoat
__ Raincoat
__ Hat
__ Scarves/wraps
__ Gloves
__ Pocketbook
__ Shoes: dress
__ Slippers

Optional Women's Clothing

__ Socks: sport

— Pants: dress/casual
— Evening clothes: gowns
— Polos/turtlenecks
— Dungarees
— Shorts
— Halters
— Sweaters/vests
— Sportswear: jogging suit/sweat band/tennis outfit/ sweat short/goggles/running bra
— Bathing suit
— Bathing suit top/robe
— Bathing cap
— Jacket/outerwear
— Stole
— Evening purse
— Boots/rubbers
— Sneakers
— Casual shoes/sandals
— Shower/beach shoes

Basic Personal Effects and Toiletries

— Toothbrush/toothpaste
— Dental Floss
— Comb/brush
— Barrettes/ribbons/rollers/clips/rubber bands/bobby pins
— Hair dryer
— Shaving gear: razor/blades/shaving cream/brush/ after-shave lotion/electric razor/cord/styptic pencil
— Shampoo
— Deodorant
— Skin lotions/cream/other toiletries/cleaners
— Perfumes/colognes
— Cosmetics: powder/rouge/lipstick/eye makeup/ compact/eyelashes/lash curler
— Mirror
— Prescribed or other medications
— Dentures/container/cleaner

__ Shower cap
__ Soap
__ Medical appliances: trusses, braces, elastic bandages

Optional Personal Effects and Toiletries

__ Wig/wig box
__ Manicure/nail equipment
__ Tweezer/scissors
__ Bleaches/depilatories/hair coloring
__ Lip balm
__ Tissues/cotton balls/toilet tissues
__ Cotton swabs
__ Sanitary pads/belt/tampons
__ Contraceptives
__ First-aid kit/thermometer
__ Aspirin/Dramamine
__ Toothpicks

Basic Accessories

__ Suitcase
__ Wallet/money clip/pocketbook
__ Money/traveler's checks/credit cards/checkbook
__ Travel tickets
__ IDs/licenses/medical insurance cards/medical alert cards
__ Date book/address book
__ Pens/papers/stationery
__ Business cards
__ Briefcase/attaché case
__ Work from office/home/correspondence
__ Directions/reservation receipts
__ Watch
__ House keys
__ Eyeglasses/extra pair/eyeglass strap/lens cleaner
__ Sunglasses
__ Contact lenses/cleaning equipment
__ Calculator

Optional Accessories

___ Diary/ledger book
___ Umbrella
___ Lighter/cigarettes/pipe gear
___ Traveling clock/alarm
___ Travel iron
___ Camera/film/flash
___ Sewing kit
___ Spot remover
___ Shoe-shine equipment/shoetrees
___ Hangers
___ Laundry bag
___ Plastic bags (for wet bathing suit, washcloth)
___ Sports gear: tennis racket/balls/skis
___ Books/games/cards/magazines
___ Personal items: pictures/good-luck charm
___ Maps/information about area
___ Radio/batteries
___ Tape recorder/tapes/earphones
___ Luggage carrier
___ Liquor
___ List for repacking

SEE ALSO:
   BEFORE YOU GO (LIST 40)
   TRAVEL ARRANGEMENTS (LIST 41)
   WHEN YOU RETURN (LIST 42)
   PREPARING/PACKING A CAR FOR A TRIP (LIST 60)

68. Packing for a Hospital Stay

If you live alone, look at Before You Go (list 40) so you can close up your home or apartment before entering the hospital.

Preparations

___ Leave valuables, jewelry at home
___ Leave medications at home/bring a list of medications currently taken
___ Inquire about hospital rules, restrictions, visiting hours
___ Prepare clothes to be brought to hospital for trip home
___ Pack

Clothes

___ Robe
___ Pajamas/nightgown
___ Slippers
___ Street clothing
___ Underwear
___ Socks

Personal Effects and Toiletries

___ Toothbrush/toothpaste
___ Comb/brush
___ Hair clips/barrettes/curlers
___ Shampoo
___ Soap
___ Shower cap

___ Shaving gear: razors/blades/shaving cream/brush/
after-shave lotion/electric razor/cord/styptic pencil
___ Mirror
___ Deodorant
___ Perfume/cologne/talcum powder
___ Cosmetics
___ Lip balm
___ Body/hand lotion
___ Manicure set
___ Tweezers
___ Dental floss
___ Tissues
___ Dentures/denture container/cleaner
___ Medical appliances: cane/brace/trusses
___ Sanitary belt/pads/tampons

Accessories

___ Suitcase
___ IDs/hospital cards/medical alert cards, tags
___ Change for phones/small amount of money/
checkbook/wallet
___ Telephone book
___ Inexpensive watch/clock
___ Pens/pencils/paper
___ Eyeglasses/case/contact lenses/cleaning equipment
___ Books/magazines
___ Puzzles/hobby projects/toys/good-luck charm/cards
___ Radio/earphones
___ Lighter/cigarettes/pipe gear
___ Television listings
___ Photos of family
___ Special pillow
___ Plastic bags for laundry to be sent home
___ Vase

For Children

___ Special animal/blanket

__ Toys/books/games
__ Night light

Maternity Stay

__ Sanitary belt
__ Open-front nightgown
__ Nursing bras/nursing pads
__ Child-care books/nursing books
__ Loose clothing to be worn home

For Natural Childbirth

__ Picture or object to focus on during labor
__ Tape or clip to mount focus object
__ Childbirth instruction booklet
__ Cornstarch/powder/lotion
__ Rolling pin or can of tennis balls for back labor
__ Washcloths
__ Mouth spray/hard candy
__ Watch with second hand
__ Lip balm/lip gloss/petroleum jelly
__ Cologne/after-bath lotion
__ Sandwich/thermos of coffee (for father)
__ Camera/film/flash
__ Eyeglasses/contact lenses
__ Tape recorder/relaxation tape
__ Champagne/plastic glasses

For Baby

(Pack items and leave at home until discharge date.)
__ Undershirt
__ Stretch suit/kimono
__ Sweater
__ Hat
__ Booties
__ Bunting

___ Receiving blanket
___ Warm blanket
___ Disposable diapers

SEE ALSO:
  EXPECTING A BABY (LIST 3)
  PREPARING THE NURSERY (LIST 4)
  AFTER THE BABY IS BORN (LIST 5)
  SERIOUS ILLNESS/HOSPITAL STAY (LIST 18)

PACKING CHECK √ LISTS
Miscellaneous

69. Dinner Party

___ Decide on date and time
___ Plan guest list
___ Write out directions to house/duplicate
___ Call guests
___ Buy invitations/buy stamps/mail invitations, directions
___ Plan menu/consider special dietary needs
___ Check recipes for procedures to be done ahead of time: marinating meats, soaking fruit in wine
___ Assess need for caterer/hire caterer
___ Assess need for hired help/hire help
___ Choose music/hire musicians
___ Arrange child care
___ Assess space requirements/arrange for adequate space
___ Borrow/rent/buy needed furniture: tables, chairs, portable bar, coat rack
___ Count/rent/borrow/buy dishes, cups, serving bowls, punchbowl
___ Count/rent/borrow/buy glasses and pitchers: wine, liquor, water, beer, parfait, punch
___ Polish/count/rent/borrow/buy silverware
___ Take out/polish silver: trays, candlesticks, bowls, candy dishes, fruit dish, coffee service
___ Take out napkin rings, salt and pepper shakers, sugar bowls, creamers
___ Clean tablecloths, napkins, dishtowels, aprons
___ Prepare/clean outfit to be worn
___ Make shopping list/include the following categories:
  a. hors d'oeuvres
  b. cocktails, drinks
  c. appetizer
  d. entree
  e. vegetables
  f. salad
  g. bread

    h. condiments
    i. nonalcoholic drinks
    j. desserts
    k. coffee, tea
    l. after-dinner candies, liqueurs

___ Get money to cover expenses

___ Buy wine, liquor, beer

___ Buy bar condiments and supplies: cherries, olives, onions, lemons, limes, oranges, stirrers, shakers, toothpicks, cocoanut, pineapple

___ Buy mixers, juices

___ Buy snack food for bar: peanuts, pretzels, crackers

___ Buy paper goods: napkins, bathroom guest towels, coasters, doilies, cocktail napkins

___ Buy film, flash

___ Shop for food

___ Make ice

___ Chill wine

___ Make list of cooking and cleaning chores

___ Prepare foods that can be made early

___ Clean house

___ Empty dishwasher/clean out dish drain

___ Put out guest towels

___ Pick up rented equipment

___ Rearrange furniture

___ Clean out hall closet/put up coat rack

___ Prepare space for boots, umbrellas, raincoats

___ Check outdoor lighting

___ Put out ashtrays, coasters

___ Make dinner plans for children

___ Buy last-minute perishables

___ Buy flowers

___ Decorate house

___ Make centerpiece

___ Load camera/take pictures of table

___ Cook

___ Arrange seating plan

___ Prepare bar/put out ice bucket, tongs, cocktail stirrers, cocktail shakers, condiments, napkins, snack food

___ Set table
___ Make juices for drinks
___ Set up coffee maker, teapot
___ Plug in coffee maker (a large one can take an hour to perk)
___ Prepare creamers, sugar bowls, lemons, tea bags
___ Set out hors d'oeuvres
___ Put out ice
___ Decant wine
___ Warm/prepare serving dishes
___ Serve drinks
___ Serve meal
___ Clear away dishes and glasses
___ Empty ashtrays
___ Clean up
___ Return rented and borrowed items
___ Record guest list, menu, table settings for future reference

70. Barbeque

This is a party list, intended for something rather more elaborate than a simple franks-and-burgers backyard barbeque.

___ Decide on date, time
___ Make rain date
___ Plan guest list
___ Write out directions to house/duplicate
___ Call guests
___ Buy invitations and stamps/mail invitations and directions
___ Plan menu
___ Make shopping list
___ Decide on who will be chef
___ Assess need for caterer/hire
___ Arrange for other help: waiters, cooks, buffet servers
___ Hire entertainment/choose music
___ Arrange child care
___ Assess space needs
___ Borrow/rent/buy charcoal grills
___ Borrow/rent/buy chairs, tables, benches, tent
___ Count/rent/buy dishes, cups and serving dishes, punch bowl
___ Count/rent/buy glasses: rock, wine, highball, beer
___ Count/rent/buy silverware
___ Take out silver items: trays, bowls, candlesticks/polish
___ Clean table linen, dishtowels, aprons
___ Take out napkin rings, salt and pepper shakers
___ Clean cooking utensils, pot holders, chef's hat
___ Prepare outfit to be worn
___ Check recipes for procedures to be done in advance: marinating meats, soaking fruit in wine

— Get money to cover expenses
— Buy liquor, beer, wine
— Buy bar condiments and supplies: cherries, olives, onions, lemons, limes, oranges, stirrers, peanuts, crackers, pretzels
— Buy mixers and juices
— Borrow/buy/rent pitchers for sangria, beer, cold drinks
— Buy candles, citronella candles
— Buy film, flash
— Buy paper goods: napkins, party plates, guest towels, doilies, cocktail napkins, tablecloths
— Buy charcoal, wood, lighter fluid, gas
— Buy condiments: mustard, ketchup, relish, pickles, mayonnaise, chili sauce, steak sauce
— Shop for other food
— Make ice
— Chill wine
— Make list of cooking and serving chores
— Prepare foods that can be cooked early
— Clean house
— Empty dishwasher/clear out dish drain
— Clear away valuables and breakables
— Put out guest towels
— Rearrange furniture/arrange candles
— Check outdoor lighting
— Clean outdoor area
— Dig barbeque pit
— Clean outdoor furniture
— Set up antibug device, citronella candles
— Protect flower beds
— Set up garbage pails
— Notify neighbors about party
— Decorate outdoor area
— Put out ashtrays, coasters
— Set up tables, chairs
— Set table
— Prepare bar
— Decant wine
— Buy last-minute perishables
— Buy flowers/arrange

- Make dinner plans for children
- Set up coffee maker and teapot
- Plug in coffee maker (large ones can take an hour to perk)
- Prepare juices for bar
- Cut fruit
- Prepare creamer, sugar bowls, tea bags
- Set out hors d'oeuvres
- Build fire
- Warm/prepare serving dishes
- Put out ice
- Serve drinks
- Cook
- Clear away glasses and dishes/empty ashtrays
- Clean up/fill in barbeque pit
- Return rented or borrowed items

71. Child's Birthday Party

___ Decide on date and time for party
___ Talk over the kinds of parties
___ Establish limits with child: number of guests, supervision
___ Decide on activities, games, entertainment, food, prizes, favors
___ Plan guest list including children, parents, family, others
___ Call guests/give directions to party
___ Buy invitations/buy stamps/mail invitations and directions
___ Plan menu
___ Make shopping list
___ Assess need for help
___ Hire entertainment/reserve facilities: skating rink, bowling alley, miniature golf course
___ Buy tickets: plays, circus
___ Assess space needs
___ Make seating plan and name cards
___ Borrow/rent chairs, tables, punch bowl
___ Polish silverware, trays
___ Clean table linen, dishtowels, aprons
___ Prepare child's outfit
___ Prepare your outfit
___ Get money to cover expenses
___ Buy birthday candles
___ Bake/order cake
___ Buy film, flash
___ Buy paper goods: plates, cups, napkins, tablecloths, paper towels, doilies
___ Buy plastic silverware, cups, garbage bags
___ Buy ice cream, candy, cake
___ Buy soda, juices, milk, coffee, tea, liquor
___ Shop for food: dinner, snacks
___ Buy/make ice

- ___ Buy thank-you notes
- ___ Buy hats, balloons, streamers, decorations
- ___ Buy gift for child
- ___ Buy prizes, favors, items needed for games, candy bags
- ___ Make list of cooking and serving chores
- ___ Clean house
- ___ Put away breakables, valuables
- ___ Rearrange furniture
- ___ Load camera
- ___ Decorate house
- ___ Buy last-minute perishables
- ___ Buy flowers
- ___ Make centerpiece
- ___ Cook
- ___ Set table/put out favors
- ___ Make juices
- ___ Set up coffee maker and teapot
- ___ Prepare creamer, sugar bowl, lemons, tea bags
- ___ Serve food
- ___ Leave time for games and activities
- ___ Clean up
- ___ Return rented/borrowed items
- ___ Send thank-you notes

72. Shower

Shower traditions vary greatly, and we suggest you discuss your ideas with friends and relatives of the guest of honor before you proceed. However, most showers still seem to include making paper plate hats from the ribbons of the gifts and recording the comments of the guest of honor.

We've divided the list into sections on a shower at home and at a restaurant or hall.

General Arrangements

___ Select date, time
___ Choose theme for shower: linen, kitchen
___ Plan guest list
___ Decide on location of shower: house, hall, restaurant
___ Hire restaurant, hall
___ Decide whether shower is to be surprise
___ Figure out how to create surprise/set up arrangements
___ Write directions to house, restaurant/duplicate for guests
___ Call guests/buy invitations/buy stamps
___ Inform guests of theme of shower and if party is surprise/ask guests to come on time and earlier than guest of honor/give directions
___ Mail invitations
___ Arrange child care
___ Get money to cover expenses/decide if group will share expenses
___ Plan outfit to be worn
___ Buy supplies: crepe paper, safety pins, paper plates, glue, balloons
___ Buy/make/borrow shower umbrella
___ Buy/make/borrow wishing well
___ Choose area for gifts
___ Buy book to record comments of guest of honor

___ Buy/make centerpiece
___ Make corsages for guests/buy gifts for guests
___ Buy gift for guest of honor/wrap
___ Buy/wrap gifts for wishing well
___ Buy film, flash

At Restaurant or Hall

___ Plan menu with staff, caterer
___ Discuss bar policies and costs with staff
___ Discuss decorations, flowers, table linens
___ Make seating plan/discuss with staff
___ Arrange for rental equipment, hired help
___ Order cake
___ Prearrange payment of bill
___ Discuss arrangements with staff if guest of honor is to be surprised

At Home

___ Plan menu
___ Make shopping list
___ Assess need for caterer/hire
___ Assess need for hired help/hire
___ Borrow/rent/buy needed items: chairs, tables, portable bar, coat rack
___ Count/rent/buy dishes, cups, serving dishes, punch bowl
___ Count/rent/buy glasses: beer, rock, wine, highball, punch
___ Count/rent/buy/polish silverware
___ Take out/polish trays, silver, candlesticks, serving dishes
___ Clean table linens, dishtowels, aprons
___ Take out napkin rings, salt and pepper shakers
___ Check recipes for procedures done ahead of time: marinating meats; soaking fruit in wine
___ Buy liquor, beer, wine

___ Buy bar condiments and supplies: cherries, olives, onions, lemons, limes, oranges, stirrers, pineapple, cocoanut

___ Buy mixers, juices

___ Buy candles

___ Buy paper goods: napkins, guest towels, doilies, cocktail napkins, coasters, tablecloths

___ Buy decorations

___ Order cake

___ Shop for food

___ Make ice

___ Chill wine

___ Make list of cooking and serving chores

___ Prepare foods that can be cooked early

___ Clean house

___ Empty dishwasher/clear out dish drain

___ Clear away breakables

___ Put out guest towels

___ Rearrange furniture

___ Prepare area for gifts

___ Clean out closets/put out coat rack

___ Prepare space for boots, umbrellas

___ Check outdoor lighting

___ Notify neighbors, police if a large party

___ Load camera

___ Put out ashtrays, coasters

___ Decorate house/put out shower items: wishing well, centerpiece

___ Buy last-minute perishables

___ Buy flowers

___ Cook

___ Set table

___ Prepare bar/put out ice bucket, tongs, cocktail shaker, bar towels, condiments, napkins, snacks

___ Make juices for drinks

___ Set up coffee maker/teapot

___ Plug in coffee maker

___ Prepare creamer, sugar bowl, tea bags, lemons

___ Put out ice

___ Set out hors d'oeuvres

— Warm/prepare serving dishes
— Give favors to guests
— Serve drinks
— Decant wine/pour
— Serve food
— Clear away glasses, dishes
— Empty ashtrays
— Clean up
— Return rented and borrowed items

73. Wedding Party at Home

Whether you do your own cooking or hire a caterer will affect how many items on this list are relevant to your needs. If you are using a caterer, review the menu carefully and find out which items you'll be responsible for—who buys the olives for the drinks or the doilies for the trays. Caterers often bring their own help to serve, but don't take it for granted—go over every detail.

If you're doing the cooking you'll probably need to make several lists of cooking and shopping chores. You'll also need help to serve, tend bar and clean up; we advise that you go over their duties with all the hired help.

If you're having a wedding at a hall, restaurant, or hotel, see Getting Married (list 2).

___ Decide on date, type, size of party: tent on lawn, cocktails, buffet, sit-down meal
___ Decide on time
___ Discuss with parents
___ Reserve church, synagogue, meeting hall
___ Check on special religious or family traditions: breaking a glass, giving favors to guests, saying a special prayer, wedding canopy, throwing rice
___ Select clergyman/discuss wedding plans, ceremony, religious issues, payment
___ Discuss responsibilities and financial details with family: who will pay for and order flowers, who will pay for band, liquor, photographer, clergyman
___ Make up guest list
___ Print invitations, direction to home, RSVP cards and envelopes, thank-you notes, announcements
___ Address invitations/buy stamps/mail invitations, directions
___ Assess needs for caterer/hire
___ Plan menu/make shopping lists
___ Assess need for hired help/hire

- Discuss liquor, champagne, bartender with caterer/ hire bartender
- Hire band/choose music for dancing, processional, service, recessional
- Decide on color scheme, accessories
- Assess space needs/rent tent, dance floor
- Rent/buy/borrow dishes, cups, serving bowls, silverware, punch bowls, tablecloths, napkins, glassware (water, wine, champagne, mixed drinks)
- Plan honeymoon/make reservations
- Prepare accommodations for out-of-town guests, children
- Select wedding party: best man, bridesmaids, matron of honor, flower girl, ring bearer
- Hire photographer/buy film, flash
- Choose gowns/arrange fittings/buy outfits
- Order veils, hats, gloves
- Order tuxedos, shirts, ties
- Buy shoes/have dyed
- Order items for religious services: prayerbooks, head coverings, sacramental wine, glass to break
- Decide who will wear flowers: wedding party, family members
- Hire florist/choose floral arrangements, bouquets, flower-girl basket, boutonnieres, corsages
- Arrange for flower deliveries
- Choose pillow for ring bearer
- Choose/buy gifts for wedding party
- Order/buy accessories: matchbooks, napkins, favors, ashtrays
- Select/order cake
- Choose/order rings
- Choose/register china patterns
- Choose/register silver patterns
- Tell close family about gifts you'd like to receive so they can respond to requests
- Discuss shower, bachelor party with family member
- Arrange bridesmaid luncheon
- Check state law about waiting time between blood test and marriage license

___ Make seating plan
___ Plan wedding rehearsal, rehearsal dinner
___ Decide how to use space: where to set up bar, dance floor, tables, buffets, pulpit
___ Polish silver candlesticks, salt shakers, cake knife, wine goblet
___ Clean/prepare table linen, dishtowels, aprons
___ Get money to cover expenses
___ Check recipes for items that can be prepared ahead of time
___ Shop or arrange for caterer to buy the following:
    a. food
    b. liquor, wine, champagne, beer
    c. mixers, juices
    d. bar condiments: cherries, olives, onions, pineapple, lemons, limes, oranges, stirrers, snack items
    e. candles
    f. paper goods: bathroom guest towels, doilies, cocktail napkins, extra toilet paper
___ Make shopping list/make list of cooking and serving chores
___ Cook items that can be prepared ahead of time/freeze
___ Arrange transportation to airport after wedding
___ Discuss toasts with best man
___ Make appointments for manicure, facial, haircut, hair coloring
___ Choose witnesses
___ Get blood test
___ Get license
___ Spray yard for insects
___ Prepare outdoor lighting
___ Buy miscellaneous personal items: underwear, garters gloves, cosmetics
___ See doctor for checkup and birth-control information
___ Have cash on hand for hired help, caterer, bartender, clergyman
___ Pack for honeymoon
___ Do final food shopping
___ Clean house/prepare kitchen for caterer
___ Clean out closet/put out coat rack

___ Prepare space for boots and umbrellas
___ Notify police and neighbors if large party
___ Arrange parking for guests
___ Decorate house/make centerpieces
___ Put away breakables
___ Rearrange furniture
___ Buy ice/chill sodas, champagne
___ Prepare bar/put out ice bucket, tongs, cocktail shaker, shot glass, condiments, snacks, glasswear, pitchers
___ Set up coffee maker, teapot
___ Put out ashtrays, coasters
___ Do final cooking chores
___ Set table
___ Warm serving dishes
___ Arrange for items to be returned
___ Make list of gifts as they are opened
___ Send thank-you notes

SEE ALSO:
   BEFORE YOU GO (LIST 40)
   TRAVEL ARRANGEMENTS (LIST 41)

74. New Year's Party

___ Set time for party
___ Plan guest list
___ Write out directions to house / duplicate
___ Call guests
___ Buy invitations / buy stamps / mail invitations, directions
___ Plan menu
___ Make shopping list
___ Assess need for caterer / hire
___ Assess need for hired help / hire
___ Hire entertainment / choose music
___ Arrange child care
___ Assess space needs / rent hall
___ Make seating plan
___ Borrow / rent / buy needed items: chairs, tables, portable bar, coat racks
___ Count / rent / buy dishes, cups, serving dishes, coffee makers, punch bowl
___ Count / rent / buy glasses: rock, wine, highball, champagne, punch
___ Count / rent / buy / polish silverware
___ Take out / polish trays, candlesticks, serving dishes
___ Clean table linen, dishtowels, aprons
___ Take out napkin rings, salt and pepper shakers
___ Prepare outfit to be worn
___ Check recipes for procedures to be done ahead of time: marinating meat, soaking fruit in wine
___ Get money to cover expenses
___ Buy liquor, beer, wine, champagne
___ Buy bar condiments and supplies: cherries, olives, onions, lemons, oranges, limes, pineapple, stirrers, crackers, peanuts, pretzels
___ Buy mixers, juices
___ Buy candles
___ Buy film, flash
___ Buy paper goods: napkins, guest towels, doilies, cocktail napkins, extra toilet paper

___ Buy hats, noise makers, confetti, blowers, streamers, balloons
___ Shop for food/buy breakfast
___ Make ice
___ Chill wine, champagne
___ Make list of cooking and serving chores
___ Prepare foods that can be cooked early
___ Clean house
___ Empty dishwasher/clear out dish drain
___ Clear away valuables, breakables
___ Put out guest towels
___ Rearrange furniture
___ Set up television for midnight viewing
___ Clean out closets/put out coat rack
___ Prepare space for boots, umbrellas
___ Check outdoor lighting
___ Notify neighbors and police if a large party
___ Arrange parking for guests
___ Load camera
___ Put out ashtrays, coasters
___ Decorate house
___ Buy last-minute perishables
___ Buy flowers
___ Make centerpiece
___ Make dinner plans for children
___ Cook
___ Set table
___ Prepare trays with champagne glasses
___ Prepare bar/put out ice bucket, tongs, cocktail shakers, bar towels, condiments, snacks, glassware
___ Make juices for drinks
___ Set up coffee maker/teapot
___ Plug in coffee maker
___ Prepare creamer, sugar bowl, tea bags, lemons
___ Put out ice
___ Set out hors d'oeuvres
___ Warm/prepare serving dishes
___ Serve drinks

___ Decant wine/pour
___ Serve food
___ Tell guests about celebration plans
___ Clear away glasses and dishes as needed
___ Empty ashtrays
___ Make breakfast
___ Make bloody marys
___ Clean up
___ Return rented and borrowed items

75. Christmas

___ Make list of religious and family traditions to be followed
___ Take children to see Santa Claus
___ Go caroling
___ Find out what children and family members want for Christmas
___ Make gift list for family, friends, children's gifts to adults, neighbors, colleagues, employees, teachers
___ Select gifts which must be ordered early
___ Buy gifts which must be mailed early
___ Take children shopping so they can pick out their presents for each other, parents, grandparents, teachers
___ Mail gifts
___ Buy remainder of gifts, including extras for those you forgot, those who drop in
___ Buy stocking stuffers
___ Buy wrapping paper, ribbons, gift cards, tape
___ Wrap gifts
___ Make card list/save for next year
___ Buy cards
___ Address cards
___ Buy stamps/mail early
___ Rearrange furniture
___ Order tree/pick up
___ Buy/hang wreath
___ Take out artificial tree/check for damage
___ Check decorations, creche, tree stand
___ Check tree lights/replace bulbs
___ Make decorations: popcorn and cranberry strings, tree ornaments
___ Buy decorations, bulbs, tinsel, hooks
___ Trim tree

__ Clean house
__ Buy/arrange holly, mistletoe, flowers, pine boughs
__ Set up candles
__ Decorate house, yard, outside of house
__ Place gifts under tree
__ Hang/stuff stockings
__ Leave snack for Santa near tree

Christmas Party

__ Decide on date, time
__ Plan guest list
__ Write out directions to house/duplicate
__ Call guests/buy stamps/send invitations, directions
__ Plan manu
__ Make shopping list
__ Order special holiday foods: goose, seafood, plum pudding
__ Assess needs for caterer, other help/hire
__ Borrow/rent/buy tables, chairs, coat rack, bar, coffee maker
__ Clean/rent/buy dishes, cups, serving dishes, punch bowl
__ Clean/rent/buy glasses: wine, highball, champagne, egg nog, punch
__ Polish/borrow/buy/rent silverware
__ Polish trays, silver items, candlesticks, candy dishes
__ Clean table linen, dishtowels, aprons
__ Take out napkin rings/refill salt and pepper shakers
__ Prepare outfit to be worn
__ Check recipes for procedures to be done in advance
__ Get money to cover expenses
__ Buy ingredients for special holiday treats: fruit cakes, relishes, cranberry wreaths, holiday cookies, holiday candies
__ Buy liquor, beer, wine
__ Replenish bar condiments and supplies: onions, olives, cherries, lemons, limes, oranges, stirrers
__ Buy mixers, juices
__ Buy candles

- Buy film, flash
- Buy paper goods: paper towels, napkins, doilies, guest towels, tablecloths
- Shop for food
- Make ice
- Chill wine, champagne
- Make list of cooking and serving chores
- Make holiday drinks: egg nog, toddies
- Prepare foods that can be made ahead of time
- Put out guest towels
- Clear out closet/set up coat rack
- Prepare place for boots, umbrellas
- Check outdoor lighting
- Load camera
- Put out ashtrays, coasters
- Buy last-minute perishables
- Buy flowers
- Make centerpiece
- Cook
- Set table
- Prepare bar/put out ice bucket, tongs, cocktail shaker, condiments, snacks
- Make juices for drinks
- Decant wine
- Set up coffee maker and teapot
- Prepare creamer, sugar bowl, lemons, tea bags
- Put out ice
- Heat up toddies
- Set out hors d'oeuvres
- Warm/prepare serving dishes
- Serve/clean as you go
- Clean up
- Return rented/borrowed items
- Give tips, gifts, thanks to appropriate people: mailman, milkman, superintendent, doorman, employees, hairdresser, paper boy
- Check after-holiday sales on Christmas cards, gifts, decorations
- Remember the needy/donate to your favorite charity

76. Passover Seder

Passover can be observed in many ways, depending on family traditions. Therefore we have not included detailed religious rituals or customs, especially those connected with preparation for the holiday. Rather, we have focused on the Seder meal itself and the preparations for it. We suggest you work up a list covering other holiday tasks based on your own religious customs.

___ Check calendar for dates of observance
___ Discuss traditions and family customs with religious leaders, family
___ Plan guest list
___ Invite guests
___ Plan menu/the seder meal usually includes the following:
  a. matzo
  b. seder plate: hard-boiled egg, bitter herb (romaine lettuce leaves or parsley), horse radish, lamb shank, chopped nuts
  c. salt water with hard-boiled eggs
  d. gefilte fish with horse radish
  e. soup
  f. matzo balls
  g. soup nuts
  h. entree
  i. vegetable
  j. side dishes
  j. side dishes
  k. salad
  l. wine
  m. drinks for children
  n. dessert
  o. tea/coffee
  p. fruit
  q. candies
  r. nuts

- __ Make shopping list
- __ Make seating plan
- __ Assess need for help/arrange for help
- __ Prepare kitchen and house for Passover/clean/change dishes, pots, foods, counters, appliances
- __ Borrow/rent needed items: chairs, tables, Haggadahs
- __ Assess need for additional dishes, silverware, glasses/borrow/buy
- __ Polish silver, candlesticks, trays, Kiddush cup, Elijah's cup
- __ Clean table linen, napkins, aprons
- __ Take out napkin rings, salt and pepper shakers, teapot
- __ Take out/clean/polish special Passover items: seder plate, wine glasses, Haggadahs, bowl for washing, matzo cover
- __ Count/buy items needed for seder: Haggadahs, yarlmulkes
- __ Prepare outfit to be worn
- __ Check recipes for procedures to be done ahead of time
- __ Get money to cover expenses
- __ Buy Passover wine
- __ Buy candles
- __ Buy paper goods: guest bathroom towels, napkins, extra toilet paper
- __ Shop for food/check "kosher for Passover" label
- __ Make ice
- __ Make list of cooking and serving chores
- __ Prepare foods that can be cooked early
- __ Empty dishwasher/clear out dish drain
- __ Put out guest towels
- __ Check outdoor lighting
- __ Rearrange furniture/make space for tables
- __ Clean out closet space for coats/prepare space for boots, umbrellas
- __ Clean/straighten house
- __ Buy last-minute perishables, flowers
- __ Set table
- __ Put out pillows for reclining
- __ Put out plates with matzo and matzo covers

___ Prepare bowl, pitcher for hand washing
___ Prepare dishes for each course and serving dishes
___ Fill Elijah's cup with wine
___ Set out candlesticks
___ Set out warming trays
___ Put out Haggadahs
___ Put out Passover wine
___ Cook/plan on estimated time for meal
___ Set up coffee maker, teapot, sugar bowl, lemons
___ Prepare dessert platters/put aside
___ Clean up
___ Return borrowed items

77. What to Have in a Kitchen

It is hard to write a complete kitchen list these days for there are always new gadgets coming on the market. We didn't include such things as electric corn poppers or a wok for stir frying, but you're more than welcome to add them or any other items you consider essential.

This list may be particularly useful for the person setting up a household for the first time.

Appliances

___ Blender/mixer
___ Can opener/knife sharpener
___ Coffee grinder
___ Food processor
___ Juicer
___ Timer
___ Toaster/toaster over
___ Waffle iron

Utensils

___ Apple corer
___ Basting brush
___ Bottle brush
___ Bottle opener/can opener/corkscrew
___ Candy thermometer
___ Cleaver
___ Colander/sieve/strainer
___ Cookie cutters

___ Egg beater/whisk
___ Food grinder
___ Food scale
___ Funnel
___ Garlic press
___ Grater/slicer
___ Juice squeezer
___ Knives: chef's/paring/fish/bread/serrated
___ Ladle
___ Long-handled fork/spatula
___ Masher
___ Matches/matchbox
___ Measuring cups
___ Measuring spoons
___ Meat thermometer/oven thermometer
___ Nutcracker/nut chopper
___ Pastry cloth
___ Pie server
___ Rolling pin
___ Scissors
___ Salad spinner
___ Sharpening stone
___ Sifter
___ Slotted spoon
___ Spatula
___ Stirring spoons/wooden spoons/carving fork
___ Storage containers/jars
___ Tongs
___ Utility brush
___ Vegetable peeler

Equipment

___ Aprons
___ Baking equipment: round and rectangular cake pans, muffin tin, loaf pans, pie plates, pastry bags and nozzles, cooling racks
___ Bread box
___ Chopping block/chopping bowl

___ Cutting board
___ Coffeepot/filters/funnel
___ Double boiler
___ Pans: frying/sauce/omelet
___ Pots/casserole dishes/Dutch oven
___ Pot holders
___ Pressure cooker
___ Roasting pans/broiling pans
___ Teapot
___ Trivets/hot plates/asbestos pad

Serving

___ Bread basket
___ Butter dish
___ Coasters
___ Dishes
___ Glasses/cups/mugs
___ Gravy boat
___ Ice bucket/tongs/cocktail shaker
___ Napkin holder/napkin rings
___ Pitchers/juice containers
___ Place mats
___ Salad bowls/salad servers
___ Salt and pepper shakers
___ Serving bowls/dishes/platters
___ Serving spoons/scoop/ladle
___ Silverware/steak knives
___ Sugar bowl/creamer
___ Tablecloth/napkins
___ Trays

Cleaning Up

___ Broom/dust pan
___ Dish drain/dish rack
___ Dishtowels
___ Garbage can

___ Mop/wringer/pail
___ Paper-towel dispenser
___ Sponges/steel wool/cleaning equipment: oven cleaner/disinfectants/wax/ammonia/cleanser
___ Storage racks/containers

Miscellaneous

___ Cookbooks/cookbook holder
___ Magnets
___ Recipe box
___ Spice rack

78. What to Have in a Tool Box

___ Apron
___ Awl
___ Center punch
___ Chisels: wood
___ C-clamps
___ Crowbar
___ Drill
___ Drill bits
___ Electrical tape
___ Extension cord: heavy duty
___ Files: wood/metal
___ Glue: all purpose/epoxy
___ Hammer: claw
___ Level
___ Machine oil
___ Metal shears
___ Nails (assorted sizes)
___ Paintbrushes
___ Paper
___ Pencil
___ Plane
___ Pliers: insulated/needle-nosed/locking
___ Pry bar
___ Putty knife
___ Rules: flexible/folding
___ Safety goggles
___ Sanding block
___ Sandpaper
___ Saws: wood/hack/keyhole

___ Screwdrivers: flathead/Phillips
___ Screws (assorted sizes)
___ Sharpening stone
___ Soap (bar) for "greasing" screws
___ Soldering iron/solder
___ Staple gun/staples
___ Stud finder
___ Tool holster
___ T-square/right angle
___ Utility knife
___ Wire strippers
___ Work gloves
___ Wrenches: adjustable/pipe/socket

79. What to Have in a Medicine Chest

We suggest you check with your physician about what medications you should have on hand in case of emergencies. It's better to have an item and never use it than to be without it during a crisis.

Drugs

___ Antacid
___ Antidiarrheal
___ Aspirin or aspirin substitutes
___ Cold medication
___ Cough syrup
___ Enema
___ Painkiller
___ Prescription medications

First Aid

___ Adhesive bandage
___ Adhesive tape
___ Antiseptic cream
___ Burn salve
___ Emetic, such as syrup of Ipecac
___ Gauze bandage
___ Mercurochrome/iodine
___ Peroxide
___ Smelling salts
___ Styptic pencil
___ Sunburn lotion

Toiletries

___ Alcohol
___ Combs/brushes
___ Contraceptives
___ Cotton balls
___ Cotton swabs
___ Cosmetics
___ Dental floss
___ Denture cream/cleanser
___ Deodorant
___ Depilatory
___ Hair conditioner
___ Hairpins/clips/barrettes/rollers/nets/rubber bands
___ Lotions/talcs/perfume/cologne
___ Mouthwash
___ Nail gear: emery boards/clippers/scissors/polish remover/polish
___ Sanitary napkins/belt
___ Shampoo
___ Shaving equipment: razor/blades/brush/cream/lather
___ Soap
___ Tampons
___ Tissues
___ Toothbrush/toothpaste

Equipment

___ Atomizer
___ Elastic bandage
___ Eyecup/eyewash
___ Safety pins
___ Scissors
___ Shower cap
___ Special equipment: syringes/douches/hypodermic needle/sterile gloves
___ Thermometer
___ Tweezer

SEE ALSO: WHAT TO HAVE IN A FIRST-AID KIT (LIST 81)

80. What to Have in a Sewing Box

___ Bias tape
___ Bobbins
___ Buttons
___ Chalk
___ Crochet hook/other tool for pulls in knitted wear
___ Darning egg
___ Elastic
___ Hem marker
___ Hemming tape
___ Hooks and eyes (assorted sizes)
___ Measuring tape
___ Needles (assorted sizes)
___ Needle container
___ Needle threader
___ Patches
___ Pattern tracing wheel
___ Pins
___ Pincushion
___ Pinking shears
___ Razor blades: single edge/thread remover
___ Safety pins
___ Seam ripper
___ Scissors
___ Sewing box
___ Thimble
___ Thread (all colors)
___ Zippers

81. What to Have in a First-Aid Kit

We suggest two ways of using this list when making your first-aid kit. First, decide what the kit is for and pick out the appropriate gear (you would want moleskin on a hiking trip but not necessarily in your workshop). Second, decide how much the kit should weigh. You want a light kit if you're going to carry it forty miles over a mountain range, but if the kit will be mounted on the wall of your workshop you can fill it up to your anxiety's content.

Consult your physician about specific antibiotics or painkillers to keep on hand.

Bandages and Tape

___ Gauze bandage
___ Sterile gauze pads
___ Triangular bandage
___ Butterfly bandage
___ Crepe bandage
___ Elastic bandage
___ Adhesive bandage
___ Adhesive plaster
___ Adhesive compress
___ Adhesive surgical tape
___ Waterproof adhesive tape
___ Moleskin/molefoam
___ Cotton wool
___ Eye dressing

Disinfectants

___ Germicidal soap
___ Antiseptic/iodine/peroxide
___ First-aid cream
___ Antiseptic wipes

Instruments

___ Needle/tweezers
___ Scissors
___ Safety pins
___ Tourniquet
___ Splints
___ Sling
___ Atomizer
___ Disposable syringe/needles
___ Thermometer
___ Antiseptic swabs
___ Space blanket
___ Snake-bite kit
___ Razor blade
___ Catheter
___ Eyecup/eyewash
___ Sterile gloves

Medication

___ Antibiotics
___ Aspirin
___ Salt tablets
___ Dramamine
___ Burn medication
___ Antidiarrheal
___ Cold medication
___ Indigestion medication
___ Laxative
___ Painkiller
___ Sunburn lotion
___ Lip balm

___ Sun screen
___ Calamine lotion
___ Smelling salts

Miscellaneous

___ First-aid book
___ Instructions/illustrations for using each item in kit
___ Instructions for Heimlich maneuver and CPR
___ Whistle
___ Change for emergency phone calls

82. What to Have in a Tackle Box

___ Bait (eggs/pork rind)
___ Bottle opener
___ Camera/film
___ Cord
___ Creel
___ Electric head lantern
___ First-aid kit
___ Fishing license
___ Flashlight
___ Flies (assorted sizes and types)
___ Floats/bobbers
___ Food container
___ Gloves
___ Hooks (assorted sizes)
___ Hook remover
___ Insect repellant
___ Jigs (assorted sizes)
___ Knife
___ Knot diagrams
___ Leaders
___ Lighter/matches
___ Line (specialized)
___ Lip balm
___ Lures (assorted types and sizes)
___ Maps of area/depth charts
___ Minnow net/pail
___ Net
___ Oil for reel
___ Pliers (needle-nosed)

___ Reel
___ Rod-holder clips
___ Rubber worms
___ Ruler
___ Scale
___ Scaler
___ Scissors
___ Sharpening stone
___ Sinkers
___ Spinners
___ Split shot
___ Stringer
___ Sunglasses
___ Sun hat/rain gear
___ Sun screen/suntan lotion
___ Swivels (snap, ball)
___ Tackle box
___ Thermometer
___ Thermos
___ Uitlity boxes for lures, hooks, sinkers

83. What to Have in a Linen Closet

___ Antimacassars/doilies
___ Bath towels
___ Bath mats
___ Beach/picnic spread
___ Beach towels
___ Bed spreads
___ Blankets
___ Blanket covers
___ Dust ruffle
___ Extra bathroom supplies: toilet paper/soap/shampoo/
    tissues
___ Guest towels
___ Hand towels
___ Heating pad
___ Laundry bag
___ Mattress cover/pad
___ Napkins
___ Pillows
___ Pillowcases
___ Placemats
___ Sachets
___ Sheets: top/fitted
___ Shower curtain
___ Tablecloths
___ Washcloths

84. What to Have in a Garden Shed

___ Antifungal spray
___ Bird deterrents
___ Bird feed
___ Bone meal
___ Bow saw
___ Bulb planter
___ Cultivator
___ Duster
___ Edger
___ Extension cord
___ Fertilizers/plant food
___ Flats
___ Flower pots
___ Garbage can/lawn bags
___ Gloves
___ Hammer
___ Hand clippers
___ Hand fork/cultivator
___ Hand hoe
___ Hand spade
___ Hand trowel
___ Hedge clippers
___ Hoe
___ Hose/nozzle
___ Humus
___ Insecticides
___ Knee pads
___ Lawn fertilizer/spreader
___ Lawn mower/gas can/funnel/oil can/cuttings bag
___ Lime

- __ Machete
- __ Mattock
- __ Notebook for entering planting dates
- __ Pails
- __ Paper/pencil
- __ Peat moss/chips/stones
- __ Peat pots/starting pots
- __ Perlite/vermiculite
- __ Pesticides
- __ Pick ax
- __ Pitchfork
- __ Planting calendar
- __ Plant pots
- __ Potting soil
- __ Pruning saw
- __ Pruning shears
- __ Rakes: metal/leaf
- __ Rubber boots
- __ Sand
- __ Screening/chicken wire
- __ Scythe
- __ Seeder
- __ Seeds
- __ Shovels: garden/snow
- __ Spade
- __ Spraying gear/mask
- __ Sprinkler
- __ Stakes/string/yarn
- __ Sun hat/visor
- __ Tiller
- __ Tree trimmer
- __ Twine
- __ Watering can
- __ Weeder
- __ Wheelbarrow

85. What to Have in a Car

Glove Compartment

___ Car manual
___ De-icer
___ Dust cloth
___ Emergency space blanker
___ First-aid kit
___ Flashlight
___ Insurance card
___ Maps
___ Paper towels
___ Service booklet
___ Tire gauge
___ Towing cards
___ Window-cleaning fluid

Trunk

___ Air pump/tire inflator
___ Chains
___ Emergency flag
___ Flares/reflectors
___ Gas can
___ Jack
___ Jumper cables
___ Oil/spout
___ Rags
___ Rope
___ Sand
___ Scraper/brush
___ Shovel
___ Snow tires

___ Spare parts (wiper blades, fan belts, fuses, bulbs)
___ Spare tire
___ Star wrench
___ Tool kit
___ Water can
___ Wax/touchup paint
___ Wedges
___ Work gloves

Personal Gear

___ Change for tolls
___ Extra car keys
___ Extra eyeglasses
___ Garbage bag
___ Gum/hard candy
___ Tissues

86. What to Have in an Office Desk

In Desk

__ Airmail paper/envelopes
__ Aspirin
__ Buttons
__ Can opener
__ Carbon paper
__ Cigarettes/matches
__ Comb/brush
__ Eating utensils
__ Emery board/nail file
__ Envelopes
__ Erasers
__ Eyeglasses (extra pair)
__ Felt-tip pens
__ File holders/separators
__ File tabs
__ Folders
__ Glue
__ Hand lotions
__ Ink
__ Interoffice envelopes
__ Makeup/cosmetics
__ Manila envelopes
__ Masking tape
__ Medications
__ Memo papers
__ Message pads
__ Mirror
__ Nail polish/polish remover

- __ Nail scissor
- __ Needle/thread
- __ Note pads
- __ Office keys
- __ Paper clips
- __ Pencils
- __ Pens
- __ Perfume/cologne
- __ Pipe gear
- __ Postcards
- __ Razor blade
- __ Rubber bands
- __ Rubber cement
- __ Ruler
- __ Safety pins
- __ Scissors
- __ Shaving equipment
- __ Snack foods: tea bags, candy
- __ Stamps
- __ Staple remover
- __ Staples
- __ Stationery
- __ Stick-on labels
- __ Stockings (extra pair)
- __ String
- __ Tampons/sanitary pads
- __ Thumb tacks
- __ Toothpicks/dental floss/toothbrush
- __ Typewriter correction paper/fluid
- __ Typewriter ribbons
- __ Typing paper

On Desk

- __ Art objects
- __ Ashtray/lighter
- __ Blotter
- __ Book ends
- __ Calendar

___ Clock
___ Desk organizer/divider
___ Dictionary/thesaurus/reference books
___ Lamp
___ Letter opener
___ Name plate
___ Paperweight
___ Pen/pencil container
___ Pencil sharpener
___ Photographs of family
___ Radio
___ Stapler
___ Telephone/address book/ring file
___ Vase
___ Zip codes

87. Food Shopping

We've ordered this list according to where you might keep the item, because when we make a shopping list we generally stand in front of the refrigerator or pantry and check on what's missing. Of course, what we keep in the refrigerator, you may keep in the cupboard.

Pantry

__ Applesauce
__ Baby food, formula
__ Bakery items: cakes, muffins, bread
__ Baking supplies: baking soda, pie crust, fillings, chocolate bits, baking powder, bitter chocolate, food coloring
__ Bar condiments: cherries, olives, onions
__ Beans, lentils: canned, dried
__ Bread crumbs, stuffing
__ Cake, frosting mixes
__ Candy, gum
__ Canned dinners: ravioli, stew, hash
__ Cereals: hot, cold
__ Cocoa, chocolate syrup
__ Cookies
__ Cornstarch
__ Crackers
__ Dietetic items
__ Drinks: juices, powdered mixes, fruit syrups
__ Ethnic foods: Chinese dinners, gefilte fish, water chestnuts, matzo, saffron
__ Extracts: vanilla, almond
__ Flour
__ Fruits: canned, dried

___ Garlic
___ Gravies, meat additives
___ Honey, molasses, syrups
___ Ice cream cones, sprinkles, dessert toppings
___ Icing, frosting
___ Instant breakfast
___ Jams, jellies
___ Milk: powdered, canned
___ Meats: canned
___ Nuts
___ Oil: salad, olive
___ Onions
___ Pancake mix
___ Peanut butter, other spreads
___ Pepper
___ Pet foods
___ Potatoes
___ Puddings, gelatins
___ Raisins
___ Rice, rice dinners
___ Salad dressing
___ Salt
___ Sauces: Worcestershire, soy, tabasco, hot, marinades, wine, sherry
___ Shortening
___ Snacks: chips, pretzels, popcorn
___ Sodas, mixers
___ Soups, bouillon
___ Spaghetti, macaroni, noodles
___ Specialty items: oysters
___ Spices, tenderizers
___ Sugar: granulated, brown, confectioner's, cubes
___ Tea
___ Tomatoes: puree, whole, paste, sauces
___ Tuna, salmon, sardines, mackerel
___ Vegetables: canned, dried
___ Vinegar
___ Water: bottled

Refrigerator and Freezer

___ Appetizers: cold cuts, salads, herring
___ Beer
___ Bread, muffins, refrigerator rolls
___ Butter, margarine, lard
___ Cheeses: grated, solid, cottage, creamed, processed, slices
___ Coffee: ground, instant, decaffeinated
___ Cream: heavy, half and half, whipped, sour, cream substitute
___ Eggs, egg substitute
___ Fish
___ Fruits: fresh, frozen
___ Frozen cakes, pies, dessert
___ Frozen dinners
___ Frozen waffles, breads
___ Ice cream
___ Juices: frozen, canned, lemon, lime
___ Ketchup
___ Maple syrup
___ Mayonnaise
___ Meats: dinner, luncheon
___ Milk
___ Mustard
___ Pickles, olives, relishes
___ Poultry
___ Sauces: barbeque, sparerib, cocktail, horse radish
___ Soda
___ Vegetables: salad, fresh, frozen
___ Yogurt

Cleaners

___ Air deodorant
___ Ammonia
___ Appliance wax
___ Bleach
___ Detergent
___ Dishwasher powder

__ Dishwashing liquid
__ Disinfectant
__ Drain cleaner
__ Fabric softener
__ Floor wax
__ Furniture polish
__ Liquid cleaners
__ Metal polish
__ Mop refills, cleaning brushes, sponges
__ Oven cleaner
__ Scouring pads
__ Scouring powder
__ Shoe polish
__ Soap: cake, liquid, powdered
__ Stain remover
__ Starch
__ Toilet cleaners
__ Window-washing liquid

Paper Goods

__ Aluminum foil
__ Foil pans
__ Freezer paper
__ Garbage bags
__ Gift wrap, ribbon, bows
__ Lunch bags
__ Masking tape
__ Napkins
__ Paper plates, cups
__ Paper towels
__ Plastic bags
__ Plastic wrap
__ Stationery, envelopes
__ Tissues
__ Toilet paper
__ Toothpicks
__ Waxpaper

Drugs

___ Adhesive bandages, gauze pads
___ Antiseptic creams, lotions, alcohol, witch hazel
___ Baby gear: diapers, shampoo, formula, creams, powder, pins
___ Bubble bath
___ Contraceptives
___ Cotton balls, pads
___ Cotton swabs
___ Dental floss
___ Deodorant
___ Hair clips, coloring, conditioner
___ Lotions: after-shave, hand, moisturizer
___ Medications· aspirin, antacids, nose drops, cough syrup
___ Mouthwash
___ Razor blades, razor
___ Sanitary pads, tampons
___ Shampoo
___ Shaving cream, soap
___ Suntan lotion, sunburn cream, sun screen
___ Toiletries: powder, cosmetics, cleansers/scent
___ Toothpaste, toothbrush
___ Vitamins

Household Items

___ Batteries
___ Charcoal briquets
___ Glue
___ Hardware/utensils
___ Insect repellent/mosquito coils
___ Lightbulbs
___ Lighter fluid
___ Matches
___ Pet Litter
___ Pet toys, bones
___ Shoelaces

__ String, twine
__ Tape

Miscellaneous

__ Cigarettes
__ Liquor, drink mixes
__ Magazines
__ Stamps, postcards, aerograms

88. Family Clothing Sizes

Article	Name	Name	Name	Name
Underpants				
Bras				
T-shirts				
Socks				
Stockings				
Slips				
Robes				
Pajamas				
Nightgowns				
Bathing suits				
Shirts (sleeve)				
Shirts (neck)				
Blouses				
Pants (waist)				
Pants (length)				
Shorts				
Skirts				
Dresses				
Sport jackets, suits				
Sweaters				
Top coats, outerware				
Belts				
Hats				
Gloves				
Shoes, boots				
Rings				